New Money Or None?

by

Willard Cantelon

Logos International
Plainfield, New Jersey

Dedicated to my sons, Lee and Paul, and the sons of all my readers who accept God's promise of a bright tomorrow

All Scripture references
are taken from the King James Version
unless otherwise noted.

NEW MONEY OR NONE?
Copyright © 1979 by Logos International
All rights reserved
Printed in the United States of America
Library of Congress Catalog Card Number: 79-90400
International Standard Book Number: 0-88270-388-9
Logos International, Plainfield, New Jersey 07060

Foreword

As a young banker in the depths of the Great Depression, one of my first assignments was that of destroying millions of dollars of currency that was tied to the gold standard.

During the forty-three years I served with the Federal Reserve Bank I witnessed many changes in the monetary world.

Today all informed men know that the Western world now stands at a financial crossroads. We are facing major changes in financial matters. All are asking, "What lies ahead?"

For over three decades Willard Cantelon, a student of both history and Bible prophecy, has with amazing accuracy predicted monetary changes long before they have come to pass. His timely book, *New Money or None?*, will prove most enlightening to all readers in every walk of life.

Ed P. Farley

Contents

1

New Deal Dollars

It became apparent that neither the farmer's misery nor the problems of the finance companies could endure indefinitely. The question was simply which would break first?
(Ernest Lindley)

In any large city there is nothing unusual about a traffic jam in the early morning rush hour, but on this January morning in Washington it was different. A flood of serious thoughts rushed through my mind. For an hour I stood by the window of my study, looking down on the endless line of cars parked on the George Washington Memorial Parkway below our home. Nothing was moving.

"The farmers," I said. "They have finally arrived and traffic today will be tied up all over the area."

For several weeks the press had warned about the approaching farmers. This was no ordinary demonstration of men coming to town by plane or car, these men were arriving on farm tractors.

Some had been on the road for many days, braving

the winter cold and snow on their journey from states as far away as Colorado, Kansas, Texas or Nebraska.

Only men in desperate straits would be willing to endure such hardships. And these men were desperate. For several years they had tasted the bitter disappointment of raising crops to sell on markets too low to provide them with any profit. Some farmers went so far as to say their loss from farming in recent times had actually eaten away the money they had saved from better days.

15,000 Lobbyists

While some referred to the farmers as "sons of the soil," they were far from being illiterate. Many had fine educations and were conversant with the main issues of the day. The farmers were well aware of the fact that the eastern banks, oil companies and large corporations employed men in Washington to influence legislation in their favor. Many of these lobbyists had once served as congressmen and senators and knew all the intricacies of government. And of course, those who had formerly served in the House or the Senate had "lifetime" privileges and knew many of the incumbents by their first names.

Although influence-peddling was frowned upon by some, the congressmen and senators looked upon the lobbyists as a necessary part of government. In a day of nuclear arms, computer technology and satellite communication, government had become so universal in scope and complicated in nature that lawmakers were prone to lean upon these lobbyists who could specialize in many fields. They had at their disposal the technical assistance of the firms which employed them. Communication lines available through the worldwide network of global corporations were generally more sophisticated and extensive than those of the government. When the issues at stake were sufficiently large, these lobbyists too had budgets of almost unlimited size at their disposal.

When major bills were being written, the inclusion of a single sentence in favor of a company or its policy could mean millions and even billions of dollars.

So each passing year the number of lobbyists continued to increase. From just a few hundred the number swelled to thousands. While only 2,000 were officially registered, it was estimated that in the past five years, the number of lobbyists had risen from 8,000 to 15,000.

The Farmer's Future

The farmers knew they could not compete with the 15,000 resident lobbyists representing high finance. But in an effort to at least present their case to the government in a stronger voice, they had come to make this concentrated plea that something be done to improve their plight.

When asked by a reporter about his optimism for improvement, one older farmer shook his head and replied, "I would like to believe our action would be effective, but I have to be realistic. Large corporations don't mind spending $200,000 a year to maintain a lobbyist office permanently in Washington. We can't stay. We can't offer the huge campaign donations like the others, nor can we offer favors in research and assistance. Our hope lies chiefly in our ability to show the legislators here in the Capitol that the state of the farmer is important. If government leaders refuse to heed our warning and refuse to take steps to correct the course we are now following, then we can promise there will be a repetition of the thirties."

There was a difference of at least thirty years between the ages of the reporter and the older farmer. The rookie reporter, fresh from school, had not learned very much about the Great Depression in his classroom studies. Textbooks in both public schools and colleges said very little about the fearful era known as the Great Depression.

But now world symptoms were suggesting another crash could happen and there was renewed concern that depression could be just ahead.

Problems Reappear

The farmers discussed problems, past and present. World War II had forced the nation to resort to a wartime economy. Following the war, the world rushed forward into a new era of computers, space exploration and jet travel. Standards of affluence had erased (for a time) any cloud of depression from postwar skies. But now the sky was becoming overcast with ominous clouds which threatened the future. The United Nations was a scene of discord. The International Monetary Fund had wandered off course and was struggling to avoid collapse. The dollar had been deliberately devalued. Inflationary fires were burning up the assets that had been saved in better years. The market was bad. While the world had inherited some new economic problems, it also faced some which seemed painfully familiar.

The Old Men Remembered
The older farmers could remember a market back in the late 1920s when prices paid for grain did not cover the cost of harvesting. Then came the collapse of the market that was followed by depression. Fruit rotted on trees; crops were plowed under while millions went hungry. Some farmhands worked for their board or for a lowly wage of a dollar a day. With wheat bringing thirty cents a bushel and a bushel of oats a dime, farmers saw their cash reserves depleted and turned to banks and mortgage companies for loans. As the borrowing continued, men offered land, homes and equipment as security to the lending institutions.

When loans reached the staggering total of over nine billion dollars, farmers were unable to pay either mortgage payments or taxes. Then came the tragic scenes of foreclosures.

Threat of Open Rebellion
When neither the law nor the "American System" protected farmers from mortgage foreclosures, they took matters into their own hands.

In many instances farmers banded together to resist the legal process of tax sales and foreclosures by intimidating bank and insurance company agents, sheriffs and judges, bidding on property being auctioned for a few cents on the dollar.

Almost anywhere in the farm belt, one could find farmers marching into capitols in such states as Nebraska, Iowa, Wisconsin and Oklahoma. They presented their grievances at courthouses and protested the loss of their farms.

In Iowa, Governor Herring appealed to all mortgage holders to withhold foreclosures until the state legislature could act. Other states took action also in an attempt to allay the farmers' open rebellion.

Fifty-six years had passed since Edward A. O'Neal, president of the American Farm Bureau Federation, delivered a solemn warning to the Senate. O'Neal, who represented the more conservative farmers from the Iowa Corn Belt, said, "Unless something is done for the American farmers, we will have a revolution in the countryside in less than twelve months."

Which Would Break First?

The farmers, however, were not the only people with problems. Insurance companies drawn on heavily for loans to policyholders and suffering from the termination of policies, were hard pressed for cash.

If they did foreclose on properties, they could only hope to sell the repossessed property for a fraction of their old first-mortgage value. It soon became apparent that neither the farmer's misery nor the problems of the finance companies could endure indefinitely. The question was simply, "Which will break first?"

The Banks Begin to Fall

By mid-February, 1933, it became apparent that the financial institutions of the nation would fall.

As financial paralysis crept over the country, Nevada was forced to declare a bank holiday in 1932. Louisiana, too, after several narrow escapes, was compelled to announce a bank holiday.

Then the total breakdown of the banking system began with the failure of the Union Guardian Trust Company of Detroit to solve its $51 million worth of problems. It was at this stage that Governor Comstock declared a bank holiday for the entire state of Michigan.

When this eight-day moratorium had ended and no way had been found to reopen the Detroit banks, even with immense loans from other agencies, panic began in earnest.

From Michigan, the banking problems began to spread to other large centers such as Chicago and New York.

On March 1, fifteen states and the District of Columbia were in a state of suspended or restricted banking. On Thursday, March 2, six additional states were forced to declare bank holidays.

President Herbert Hoover took no course of action. He was hoping to keep the banking system from total collapse at least until Saturday, March 4, when he could hand this problem over to his successor, President Franklin D. Roosevelt.

Roosevelt vs. New York Bankers

It was apparent that the bankers of New York

feared the philosophies of Mr. Roosevelt. Even before he assumed office on March 4, Thomas Lamont of J.P. Morgan and Company telephoned Mr. Roosevelt and recommended on behalf of the New York bankers that he take no immediate action. Governors Lehman of New York and Horner of Illinois were apparently caught between the contrasting opinions of the bankers and the president. But when the governors announced a two-day bank holiday in their states, it was obvious they were doing so at the advice of Franklin Roosevelt. On assuming office, Mr. Roosevelt took action. He ordered a national bank holiday for all the banks of the nation.

When the President Had Only $8.00

In his book, *Rendezvous with Destiny*, Elliott Roosevelt, the son of FDR, tells with a touch of humor how he was en route to California when his father ordered the closing of the banks.

In Little Rock, Arkansas, Elliott ran out of money and of course could not find a bank open to cash a check. When he phoned the White House and explained his problem to his father, the president told his son that his own cash totaled $8.00 and that Elliott would just have to do the best he could until the banks opened.[1]

Vanishing Gold

In viewing the chaotic condition of the country, Roosevelt turned his attention to gold. He was aware of the fact that astute Americans who had reason to fear that their country would be taken off the gold standard were turning in dollars for gold. This demand for gold had been especially heavy in October of 1931 and June of 1932.

More alarming, however, than the gold being hoarded by the citizens of the nation, was the flow of gold back to European nations. So two days after his assuming office as president, Mr. Roosevelt ordered an embargo on gold that would restrict the shipments to foreign lands.

As the dollar continued to fall, bankers in New York appealed for licenses to ship more gold to Europe. They declared that only small shipments would be sufficient to strengthen the dollar on the world market. Mr. Roosevelt acquiesced and lifted the embargo and in a few days America lost another $100 million in gold. The president declared this could not continue.

Trading With the Enemy Act

In seeking for power to act on this important matter, the president turned to his retired banker friend, René Léon, and asked if any of the old wartime statutes were still alive. In response to this inquiry, Leon presented the president with a transcript of the Trading with the Enemy Act of 1919, designed to prevent gold from reaching enemy nations.

When the president asked Attorney General-designate Walsh if this could be legally enforced, Senator Walsh replied that even though he had his doubts about it, he would rule it to be valid if the president required such power for the emergency [2]

America Leaves the Gold Standard

When Roosevelt presented this emergency bill, Bertrand H. Snell, the Republican floor leader, rose and said that the president was the man responsible in the crisis and it was time to follow his leadership. In spite of the fact that few leaders had even seen the emergency bill, the cries of "Vote, vote!" drowned out the few voices calling for debate. Within thirty-eight minutes after its presentation the bill passed the House by acclamation without reference to any committee and went on to the Senate. By invoking the Trading with the Enemy Act, Mr. Roosevelt not only placed an embargo on the foreign shipments at the time, but also demanded the gold from the people as well.

For anyone failing to comply with his order, penalties could be imposed in maximum sentences of $10,000 in fines and ten years of imprisonment.

Banks That Chose Bankruptcy

The hours that preceded these momentous decisions were filled with activity; conferences ran night and day.

Those in favor of a unified banking system wanted to seize the opportunity when the banks were closed to force all forty-eight-state banking systems into the Federal Reserve System.

In response to this suggestion, Senator Huey Long made a fiery appeal in favor of retaining the independence of the small bankers.

Carter Glass responded to Long's appeal with scorn and talked with contempt about the "little corner grocery men who ran banks."

Those sharing the views of Carter Glass actually preferred the permanent closing of all banks that would not affiliate with the Federal Reserve.

When the time came to reopen the banks, pitiful pleas came from many small bankers for licensure that was denied them under the new rules.

Some actually chose bankruptcy instead of joining the Federal Reserve and "relinquishing their freedoms."

According to the records, 5,000 banks never did open their doors to the public again.[3]

Printing Press Money

One banker who succeeded in keeping his bank open in those trying hours was Marriner Eccles.

As the banking crisis reached its peak, Marriner Eccles studied the people crowding anxiously into his bank. Some had stood outside for hours waiting for the doors to open. They feared that those same doors when closed at the end of the day would never open again. Reports from across the nation told of massive bank failures.

Each customer wore the same anxious expression and held a bank book in nervous hands, showing the amounts he had deposited in savings. All hoped against hope that they would be able to withdraw these funds before it was too late.

Eccles was aware of the gravity of the hour and was determined to do all in his power to keep his bank from going under.

Early that morning he had called his staff to a back room and outlined his strategy.

Count the Money as Slowly as Possible

They were, under no conditions, to leave their teller's wickets. Even at the lunch hour they were to eat a sandwich while they worked. They must not allow for one moment any slight suspicion that they were leaving their windows.

In spite of the tension, he told his employees to act relaxed and treat every customer with as much congeniality as possible.

Most important of all, they were to do everything in their power to buy time. When serving even the best known customers, they were to carefully look up their records. And when paying out funds, they were to use the smallest denominations possible and count the money very slowly.[4]

After Marriner Eccles became governor of the Federal Reserve Board, Wright Patman, chairman of Banking and Currency, asked, "How did you get the money to buy those two billion dollars worth of government securities in 1933?"

"We created it," replied Mr. Eccles.

"Out of what?" asked Patman.

"Out of the right to issue credit money," was the answer.

"And there is nothing behind it, is there, except our

government's credit?"

"Well, that is what our money is," replied Marriner Eccles.[5]

No Longer Redeemable in Gold

America had been on the gold standard since 1870. It was a momentous hour when this was changed. While the banking system of the nation was in a prostrate form, suggestions for remedy came from various sources.

When some suggested the printing of script, Bill Woodin, secretary of the treasury, opposed such a thought; he recommended that the printing presses be set in motion to run night and day, if necessary They were to print as much money as possible against the sound assets of banks. He also advocated government control over banks without a guarantee of deposits.

One little phrase was to be printed on American bills after the departure from the gold standard that would alter the course of America and the world. No longer would the dollar read, "Redeemable in gold." It would now read, "Redeemable in lawful money."

My friend, Edwin Farley, a young banker in those days, told me of his unpleasant task of destroying millions of bills which read, "Redeemable in gold on demand from the United States Treasury."

Inflation Worth a Try

When the president demanded that the gold be submitted to the government at $20.67 an ounce, the

13

people had no alternative other than to comply. Nor did they have any say in the price they received for their gold, nor the new price that was immediately raised to $35.00 an ounce. By increasing the price of gold in this manner, the government realized an immediate profit. Such an act, of course, was one of deliberate inflation of the dollar. Mr. Roosevelt was well aware of this and said,

> Inflation is worth a try; it might work like a shot of adrenalin to stimulate the heartbeat of the economy. A sure-fire method of forcing up prices would be to devalue the dollar.[6]

The man who influenced Roosevelt greatly in this radical decision was the British economist John Maynard Keynes. He referred to gold as "barbarous metal," and advocated deficit spending to cure the depression.

It Produced Stagflation

The theories of Keynes brought temporary relief but long-range tragedy. Leonard Silk wrote of this in the *New York Times*. He implied that our present-day chronic inflation results largely from acceptance of the policies of Keynes.[7]

In Brussels I picked up a copy of *Time* magazine and read that economists are in agreement that the old ideas do not work in attempting to control stagflation. They point out that the Keynesian idea of counter-acting depression with a stiff dose of government spending leads to inflation.[8]

James Dines also believed the present problems could be traced back to their origin in the thirties. He said,

> Today's crisis has been building since 1933. There has been no precedent for such monetary instability in the financial history of the world. The man on the street has no concept of the financial panic and liquidity crisis which could lie just before us.[9]

They Are Moving—But Where?

The sound of traffic moving on the parkway caused me to turn once more to the window. I watched the long procession of cars creep forward. Some drivers were heading for the nearby Pentagon, others would cross the Potomac to the government buildings in the district.

"They are moving," I said to myself as I turned to the desk. "They are moving—but where?"

John Kenneth Galbraith in his book, *The Crash of 1929*, reminded his readers of the strange manner in which history had a way of being repeated in cycles. Was this another era like the thirties?

Could this demonstration of the farmers be followed with a collapse of our economic system as in the past? There were strong indications suggesting that this could well be the case. Some writers believed the cycle had already begun. Roosevelt removed the dollar from the gold standard and Mr. Nixon in 1971 removed the backing of gold from the dollar. Mr. Roosevelt raised the price of gold and Mr. Nixon did the same. Mr. Roosevelt was influenced by Keynes, and Mr. Nixon said, "I am a Keynesian." Under both administrations the raising of the price of gold caused deliberate inflation. Now the fear was that inflation—if not controlled—would collapse the economy of the Western world. What did the future hold?

2

A Dollar's Final Farewell to Gold

The greatest story of the nation, if people would listen to arithmetic, is the one that explains that in actuarial terms the Federal Government is broke. (James Davidson)

The Loss of American Gold

Between the years of 1960 and 1970, American gold reserves fell from over $17 billion to approximately $11 billion. In the same period, European nations were increasing their supplies of gold in the following amounts:

France increased her supply of gold 115 percent. Germany increased her supply of gold 34 percent. Italy increased her supply of gold 21 percent. Switzerland increased her supply of gold 25 percent. Portugal increased her supply of gold 63 percent. Belgium increased her supply of gold 23 percent. Denmark increased her supply of gold 40 percent.

As Europeans continued to exchange their undesired American dollars for the preferable gold, Mr. Nixon realized this could not continue. In a manner reminiscent of Roosevelt's action in the thirties, Mr. Nixon announced the removal of the last degree of gold backing from the American dollar. The decision was made in the meeting at the Smithsonian Institution on December 18, 1971. Not only would the dollar no longer be backed by gold, but the price of gold was to be raised to $38 an ounce which automatically devalued the dollar 8.5 percent. Mr. Nixon referred to this as the most significant monetary agreement in the history of the world.[10]

Three days prior to the announcement of the devaluation of the dollar, John Connally, secretary of the treasury, was quoted as saying,

The devaluation of the dollar would be very, very beneficial to the United States.

Facts at a later date, however, seemed to suggest that the predictions of the pundits were wrong. The devalued dollar did not induce Americans to buy less foreign products and foreigners more from America as expected.

In 1971, preceding the devaluation of the dollar, the trade deficit was approximately $2 billion.

In 1972, the year following the devaluation, it had increased to $6.4 billion.

Mr. Connally further stated that the results of the devaluation would be so mild, "I don't think the

average American will even be conscious of it."[11]
But the results were far from mild.

A Monetary System That Had Crumbled
Soon after Mr. Nixon announced the removal of
gold backing of the dollar and the increase in the
price of gold, Peter Beter said,

The currencies of Western Europe went adrift
in a sea of confusion. Dollars flowed into the
central banks of Europe. The bankers closed
their doors. The dollar was afloat.[12]

Magazines of Europe depicted on their covers
various pictures describing the devalued dollar. One
showed the dollar like a ship sinking at sea. We were
living in Europe at the time and recalled some of the
dramatic moments of 1971. There were the days
between August 11 and August 18 when European
banks refused to accept or exchange any American
dollars. Even a beggar on the steps of a church in
Paris had scrawled on a card attached to his
outstretched hat, "Dollars not wanted."

Europe Shocked Over the Announcement
Europeans were stunned by the announcement of
the devalued dollar. They had heard President John
Kennedy say,

I want to make it clear . . . that this nation will
maintain the dollar as good as gold.[13]

They had heard Mr. Kennedy's successor, President Johnson, reaffirm in his State of the Union speech on January 4, 1965,

The soundness of the dollar is unquestioned. I pledge to keep it that way.

They had believed the words of Secretary of the Treasury Henry Fowler, who said,

The dollar is not going to be devalued. The price of gold will not be raised in my lifetime as secretary.[14]

The Monetary System Continued to Crumble
In discussing his part in the devaluation of the dollar, Mr. Connally, secretary of the treasury, was quoted as saying,

If I reflected impatience it was the expression of an irresistible urge to speed up the process of altering a monetary system that had crumbled.[15]

In May of 1972, Mr. Connally resigned as secretary of the treasury. Four months after his resignation, Paul Volcker, under secretary of the Treasury for Monetary Affairs, declared in the strongest possible language,

The official price of gold would not be raised

above $38.00 an ounce.[16]

The Dollar Continues to Crumble

In spite of Mr. Volcker's announcement, another devaluation occurred in about six months. The newspapers informed us that the United States had put a 10 percent devaluation of the dollar into effect. It was predicted that the price of gold would increase from $38.00 an ounce to $42.22 an ounce.[17]

While the promises made by presidents and secretaries of the treasury were made in sincerity, they were powerless to stop the decline of the dollar.

Paper Gold

Before World War II ended members of twenty-nine nations met to form an International Monetary Fund that would be attached to the United Nations. Soon the number swelled to forty-four and on to a hundred, and continued to grow until most of the nations of the free world were members of what came to be known as the IMF.

Following the trend of the day, however, nations, like individuals, began to live so far beyond their means that the old currencies were totally inadequate to meet modern demands.

In the Rio conference of the IMF in 1967, it was suggested that "ersatz" or "substitute" money be created. And one year later in 1968 the new substitute money was introduced under the attractive name of "paper gold."

Paper gold was a misnomer, however, for the new

system was neither paper nor gold; it was merely a number system. Each member nation was allowed to draw a stipulated amount under an arrangement known as "special drawing rights."

When the announcement was made concerning paper gold, Fritz Machlup of Princeton was quoted as saying, "SDRs are becoming a new international money."[18]

While some economists in more confidential circles predicted this system heralded the new pattern for individuals as well as nations in the future, many Europeans who were alarmed by the announcement stormed the banks in cities such as London and Paris to purchase gold. Many feared that paper gold marked the immediate collapse of paper currencies.

Disorderly groups comprised of peasants and prosperous businessmen surged almost hysterically to bank windows to obtain gold. On a single day (March 14, 1968), gold hoarders took 400 tons of gold from the gold pool.

Europeans had ample reason for concern lest their paper money be suddenly rendered worthless. Germans recalled the collapse of their marks in both 1923 and 1948.

At the dawn of the seventies I had heard leaders of the Common Market declare their intention to cancel the currencies of Europe in favor of establishing a new "single" money system.

As the desire for gold increased, so did the price of the precious metal.

A "Gold Rush" in 1975 Would Have
Been Fatal to U.S. Banks

As Americans watched their European neighbors bent on hoarding gold, some asked, "When will Americans be allowed this privilege that was taken from them in 1934?"

To that query I would reply, "When the price of gold rises beyond $100 an ounce, once again you will be allowed to purchase gold."

This day came in 1975.

After being denied the right to purchase gold for almost forty-two years, the announcement was made at the close of 1974 that Americans once again would be allowed to buy gold.

The important question on the minds of many economists was, "Would there be a major run on banks by those drawing funds from savings to buy gold?"

Men conversant with the condition of American banks realized such a move could collapse many of the nation's banks.

Banks Could Have Closed in 1975

At the close of the 1950s, the banks of the nation had over 50 percent of their customers' money in their vaults. When the ban on gold ownership was lifted at the close of 1974, some banks had as little as 10 percent. If more than 10 percent of those with deposits had sought to draw money from their banks to buy gold, they would have found, to their dismay, that there was insufficient money in the banks to sustain such withdrawals. Bank failures would have been nationwide.

Could the FDIC Have Saved Us?

The Federal Deposit Insurance Corporation (FDIC) which guarantees protection on accounts up to $40,000 would have been of little help. While they could boast of success in the years of the FDIC's existence, there had been no major crisis of this nature since its inception. Some knowledgeable bankers said that the FDIC had only sufficient funds to cover about one percent of the nation's bank deposits. In other words, they could cover only about one percent of bank failures, but no more. When the days of crisis passed and banks survived, many asked, "Why did Americans not make a stronger move toward buying gold?"

The Press Was Filled With Warnings

Warnings in the press helped to avert bank failures. "Caution" seemed to be the major note of emphasis. Engelhard, the largest refiner and fabricator of precious metals in the United States, ran a full page notice in the *Los Angeles Times* on December 13, 1974. Among the many words of advice and caution, there were comments such as,

Selling gold at short intervals in the hope of making speculative profits can be full of dangers.[19]

24

There were even warnings against the dangers of counterfeiting. An additional comment from Engelhard read,

It must be recognized that gold (and any other refiner's stamp) is subject to the danger of counterfeiting. This is particularly true once gold has left the physical possession of the financial institution.[20]

As the ban was about to lift, tension prevailed in institutions as leaders watched the zero hour approaching. One headline read, " '75 Gold Rush, Brokers and Dealers Dig In."

Virginia Knauer, the president's consumer advisor, wrote: "Don't let gold dust blind your vision."

A subtitle read, "Buyers issued warning."

There were, however, some contradictory views. William Simon, secretary of the treasury, spoke in favor of lifting the ban on private ownership of gold.[21] And George Burns of the Federal Reserve opposed it.[22]

Why Did the Gold Rush Not Take Place?

Many economists, especially in Europe, were amazed that Americans did not make a rush on banks to buy gold. Some asked, "Why?"

Was it because of the massive propaganda of the press? Was it the memory of the Roosevelt Era when gold was demanded by the government at a price over which the people had no control? Or was it the grace of God that caused Americans to act with restraint and avert a domino closing of banks of the nation? Bankers at least could say, "Thank God we passed that crisis." But when would another one arise?

In the Event of Another Crash

"In the event of another crash," some asked, "what could the government do?" Mr. Roosevelt was able to realize a profit of $3 billion by collecting the people's gold. But today the people have little gold for the government to collect. In viewing the gravity of the hour, many economists drew attention to the fact that the only money the government could rely on was what it collected from the people in taxes.

The Brewing Tax Revolt

1978 was known as the year of the "tax revolt." In July, *Nation's Business* showed a taxpayer on its cover who was standing in front of his house on which was hung a large banner showing how his property tax in six years had risen from $1,318 to $6,700.

Regarding the tax revolt that began in the summer of 1978, Milton Friedman said,

The "brewing" tax revolt is no longer brewing, it is boiling over.[23]

Jason Boe, president of the National Council of

State Legislatures, in discussing the tax revolt in America, told a congressional hearing, "The Federal government is the ultimate target."[24]

And if the nation faced a major recession, it might not merely be a case of the public not willing to pay taxes, but rather a case of their inability to pay.

The time-payment debt of the American public was in excess of $190 billion. Added to this was their present obligation to the government's debt which averaged more than $4,000 for every individual in the nation.

When the stock market crashed in 1929, 30 percent of the nation's laboring force was thrown out of work. In the South men picked a hundred pounds of cotton for thirty cents and in the North they shoveled a ton of coal for twenty cents. There were actually more people on relief in those days than there were people paying taxes.

5,000 Piles of Silver Dollars
as High as the Empire State

President Roosevelt launched relief programs which plunged the nation into a debt in the billions of dollars. With the possibility of the recurrence of another depression, men asked, "How could any more debt be carried by the government of today?"

If America's debt were now to be paid in silver dollars it would require 5,000 piles of dollars as high as the Empire State Building in New York.

If the debt were paid with dollar bills it would

require a chain of dollar bills wrapped around the world 3,750 times.

"U.S. Is Broke," Taxpayers Union Chief Says

On February 1, 1978, the *Washington Star* carried the picture of James Davidson, the head of the National Taxpayer's Union and his comments concerning the nation's debt.

In utilizing statistics from the treasury and commerce clearinghouse, Mr. Davidson claimed that the actuarial debt of the nation was $7.6 trillion, which he said was equal to the value of everything in the United States. He spoke of how we have promised everything away. Social Security and other annuity programs are trillions in the red; "the country's assets are merely the claim on the taxpayer's money."[25]

The interest alone on the national debt costs the taxpayers a million dollars every twelve minutes.

The Future Could Be Devastating

Charles Warren, chairman of President Carter's Council of Environmental Quality and former California assemblyman from Los Angeles, remarked about the future of the economy: "It will be devastating . . . absolutely terrifying."[26]

With statements of this nature filling the front pages of the nation's press I asked myself, "Who does it affect more, the young who peer anxiously into the future, or the aged who want relief today from the plague of inflation that devours their early life's savings?" Retired citizens had special cause for concern.

When *Reader's Digest* ran a feature article questioning the survival of Social Security, the elderly in cities like New York and Chicago were so aroused they picketed the offices of the publisher. But each was wondering what the fate of Social Security would be.

The Insecure Dollar

In describing the Social Security program, one writer stated that the system was corrupting itself. As it is propelled into greater and greater endeavors, the writer implied, it experiences greater problems. He portrayed the frustrations of a "government gone awry."[27]

As the dollar continued to diminish in value, elderly people suffered the most. Men who spent their lives earning money for retirement observed with anguish the buying power of their dollars becoming weaker.

In the days of the Depression, when men had to turn to the government for aid, they seemed to say, "We will give you our dollars if you will protect us." As time passed, politicians offered bigger programs of care in exchange for votes. Government grew to the extent that finally one of six laborers in America was on the government's payroll. The cost of administering the welfare programs became astronomical. The government's total annual payroll exceeded $70 billion.

Mistakes Coming Home

In depicting the trend of the day, an artist portrayed a politician shoveling dollar bills into a huge hopper; this picture appeared on the cover of *U.S. News & World Report*. Those dollars were being grabbed by people representing every walk of life. The caption over the picture read:

SOCIAL SECURITY . . . WILL IT BE
THERE WHEN YOU NEED IT?[28]

Social Insecurity

I recalled the first income tax forms I submitted in 1942. Mel Jackson, a retired officer of Armour Company, offered to assist me with that first return. When questioned concerning my Social Security, I told him that as long as it was my privilege to choose not to take it, I had no intention of accepting it.

"And why would you willfully decline accepting Social Security?" he asked with curiosity.

"For three reasons," I replied promptly. "First of all, you have no choice about what you are told to pay in, and neither do you know what you will get in return. And last, but not least, Mr. Jackson," I added, "when I am old enough to receive Social Security, I am of the opinion that this system will no longer exist."

Jackson raised his brows in an expression of surprise and asked why I felt that way.

"Because," I continued, "one can prove mathematically that the system can never survive on the principles on which it was first founded."

No More Money Back Guarantees

Social Security became law on August 14, 1935. The stock market had crashed and the Great Depression had begun six years previously.

The original Social Security tax, however, was only one percent of the first $3,000 earned. That meant that no one, according to the original law, could pay more than $30.00 a year. The law at that time also guaranteed that each contributor would receive from the government as much money as he had paid into the Social Security program.

Four years after this law was passed, it was obvious that the promise of the government could never be kept, so the "money back promise" was canceled. And the limit on the premium was also changed. Thirty-three years later, it had been increased over 1,000 percent.

The cycle of demands of people and promises of politicians soon started a round of escalation that was certain to lead eventually to the breaking point.

During the first year of Dwight D. Eisenhower's administration, the Social Security budget was $3.4 billion. By 1965, it was $15.5 billion. By 1978, it was $133 billion.

Every day, 20,000 new claims were added. Every night, the complete Social Security file of wages, contained on 220,000 reels of tape, were run through computers to provide information on the claimants.

In 1978 the government spent $3.5 billion on

regulatory programs. This was an increase of 21 percent over the year before. These rules filled 60,000 pages.

Inflation Threatens Social Security's Future

From a Social Security service department in Washington one member said if inflation continued to increase at its present rate, by the year 2050 a loaf of bread would cost $37.00, a newspaper or telephone call would be $9.50, a $4,500 automobile would cost $281,000 and a $55,000 home would be $3,400,000.

Artists and cartoonists of the news media seemed to vie with one another in an effort to portray to the public the dangers of inflation. One rather gloomy creation covering a half-page in *Newsweek* showed the White House at night. Above the White House was the statement,

What will we do now, Mr. President . . . nothing seems to work?[29]

George Newman, writing in the *Sunday Mercury News,* quoted a laborer as saying,

All I know is that *I* have had six pay raises in the past five years and I am still breaking my neck to stay even.[30]

Writers in *Time,* discussing the rise in real estate prices, spoke of an engineer in New Jersey who moved to California. After selling his home in the East for $80,000, he found a comparable house in California which cost $180,000.[31]

In analyzing the wage spiral, records revealed that a laborer earning $5,000 in 1965, would have to earn $16,029 in 1985, in order to remain on the same living standard. By the same measurement, one earning $10,000 would have to earn $32,781.[32]

U.S. News & World Report ran feature articles with headlines such as, "Prices Are Soaring Ever Higher, Defying the Efforts to Cure the Nation's Worst Malady."[33]

In Europe, the *International Herald Tribune* carried one simple short announcement on a full page,

Anyone who is not mildly panicked about the inflation outlook for the U.S.A. does not recognize the seriousness of the situation.

Bill Kester quoted Henry Wallich as saying,

. . . Inflation is a means by which the strong can more effectively exploit the weak. The well organized gain at the expense of the unorganized and aged.[34]

One man who had made a thorough study of Social Security was Abraham Ellis, an English-born attorney, who practiced law in Manhattan. He was a graduate of the City College of New York and

Brooklyn Law School. His book, published by Arlington House, was entitled, *The Social Security Fraud.* In his 200 pages of outspokenness, he quotes statistics which seem irrefutable:

> We have already seen that there is virtually no cash in the so-called Social Security trust or reserve fund. It is full of I.O.U.'s with no collateral other than the taxing power to back them up. It is hard to conceive of a more hopelessly bankrupt organization than the Social Security System. . . . It is a simple fact that the State has nothing, and therefore cannot give to the people what it first doesn't take from them.[35]

Some blamed the government for too much bureaucracy but others blamed the people for expecting the government to provide more than it could afford. With the "buy now and pay later" mode of living, the "payday" was rapidly approaching when there would be no more credit extended.

Back in the 1960s, George Humphrey, secretary of the treasury, said,

> Unless the nation balanced its books there would be a depression that would curl man's hair to think about.[36]

Others of like stature suggested the next depression would make the one of the thirties look like

34

prosperity. Most people ignored these warnings which came in the sixties, but now many new voices are beginning to swell with the prediction of a coming crash

3

The Dictator's Dollars

America is headed for a crash simply because all the causes for a financial crash are already in place. Every economic principle says that it should be worse than the one of 1929.

(Harry Browne)

As I listened to the many voices predicting another crash and depression equal to, if not greater than, the Great Depression of the 1930s, my thoughts turned back to those days.

On the bookshelf near my desk was one of America's respected news magazines, containing many pictures of the Great Depression. Picking it up, I walked to the window and stood for some moments turning the pages that brought back many memories of depression days.

Memories of the Great Depression

The first picture was that of hundreds of men on top of a freight car. They did not look like ordinary men. Huddled atop the boxcars of the freight train, they resembled blackbirds clinging to a precarious perch.

The writer said,

> Farmers working in nearby fields never troubled
> to turn their heads to study the strange freight-
> turned-passenger train. Nor did those working
> in gardens adjoining the train tracks bother to
> look up when the long train of cars loaded with
> men rattled by.

This scene from the Great Depression had become all
too common in the days of the 1930s. One freight crew
estimated it hauled appoximately 180,000 men
across the States in one season.

These were men who once drove their own cars
down the highway, or rode first class in the cushioned
seats of the passenger trains which bore them in
comfort to their desired destinations. Now, without
any money for gasoline or train tickets, they had no
other mode of travel than to ride the freights, exposed
to sun, wind and rain, as they went from state to state
in search of work. There were thousands of them,
hundreds of thousands, desperate to find any place of
work that would provide at least enough money for
daily bread for themselves and their wives and kids
back home.

Slowly I turned the magazine's pages and studied
the next picture. It too showed travelers, but these
were of a different sort. They were in automobiles, if
indeed the word "automobile" did not flatter these
jalopies which were laden down with boxes and bed-
ding and all of the family brood.

The writer said this too was a common sight in depression days. Families who lost homes or farms because of inability to make payments took to the road in their family "flivvers," carrying with them the only remains of their possessions that were free from mortgages, and could be called their own.

Too Proud to Take the Dole

On the streets of New York, the photographer showed middle-aged men kneeling on the hot, dirty pavements, shining shoes. These, unlike the usual bootblacks, out to make a dollar after school, had been clerks and accountants in large firms. These men were willing to clean the shoes of a passing stranger for only a nickel.

"Eventually, however," said the writer, "when the shoeshine business failed to provide even a meager existence, more and more of these men submitted to relief."

Depression Is Like War

As I stood by the window in silence, I finally said to myself, "No writer is capable of depicting the depths of tragedy that gripped America in the days known as the Great Depression. It is like war. Men write about battles, they show scenes of struggles and conflicts and quote statistics, but they are totally incapable of portraying war in its grim reality. How can words carry the sounds of bursting shells, weeping mothers, groaning men and crying children? How can a camera look into the heart of a lad who lost his limbs in battle and knows he will never skate, ski or run again? How can paper or ink convey the heartache of a father sitting by the little cross that marks the grave of his only son? No! No! It cannot be done."

Bombs may destroy homes, but depression can rob men of their homes too, often in a slow and agonizing manner. Men die on battlefields, but in depression something within man dies. Heads once held high with pride bow in shame. Men look upon wives and children for whom they provided, and confess they are no longer able to care for those they love. So what do they do? They line up in bread lines waiting for a handout, or queue up at some soup kitchen or relief agency seeking a dole. In times of war, men don smart uniforms and march in orderly columns to the beat of drums. They march together under waving banners. Some return from scenes of action to reenlist as career soldiers. In depression, there is an awful parallel. The attire worn by millions is not the khaki or air force blue; it is the ill-fitting, mismatched clothing from some commissary. The spirit and morale of the work gangs are extremely low, for within their hearts all pride and manhood have virtually died.

The Country Yearned for a Messiah
Franklin Roosevelt was governor of New York when the Great Depression struck the land. He had seen sights like the jungle camps on the edge of the city where men without money fashioned crude shelters out of old cartons and shingled the roofs of the same with flattened tin cans. Roosevelt determined if he

was elected president he would help those who suffered.

When he took office he asked for total power to deal with the nation's monetary crisis. It soon became evident that most of the nation, including the majority in government, were willing to grant him even more power than he asked. In writing on the Roosevelt Revolution, Ernest Lindley concluded, "The country yearned for a Messiah."[37]

The Whole Credit Structure Was Sure to Collapse

When he assumed office in 1933, Mr. Roosevelt was convinced that the prices of farm products had to be raised or the whole credit structure would be certain to collapse.

It was agreed that the way to accomplish the raising of prices was to reduce production.

Under the AAA (Agriculture Assistance Act), 22,000 agents blanketed the South. In a single two-week campaign, 10,324,000 acres were taken out of production. It was a dramatic moment in American history when the cotton growers of the South were induced to plow under one quarter of their acreage.

The second great crop reduction program of the AAA was wheat. Despite a short American wheat crop in 1932 the carry-over was approximately 360,000,000 bushels, nearly three times the normal. Because markets had fallen, wheat exports had dropped from the old level of nearly 200 million bushels to about 40 million bushels.

Secretary of Agriculture Henry Wallace was determined to seek a 15 percent reduction in wheat. This meant taking 9,600,000 acres out of production.

Then came the reduction of hogs. The AAA spent $50 million in buying pigs and sows with the intention of processing them for distribution to the unemployed through the Federal Emergency Relief Administration. The plan was to buy 4 million piglets and 1 million sows. Secretary Wallace also declared his intention to take at least 10,000,000 acres of corn out of production, and to reduce the hog production by one-quarter.[38]

The plan to distribute the slaughtered pigs in the form of food to the needy proved unsuccessful. Packing centers told of most of the pigs being ground up for fertilizer, and when the storage facilities were exhausted all but a few remaining parts had to be dumped.[39]

Don't Shoot the Farmer

While farmers realized market prices should be raised, many were critical of the methods used by the government to accomplish this end.

As a lad, I overheard some of the native sons in North Dakota discussing their plight. One, who had a sense of humor, told of the government inspector coming to his farm to take inventory and issue orders concerning his acreage and stock. He said, "When my old billy goat came around from the back of the barn, the government agent went racing for the house. He dialed Washington. 'Give me Tugwell or Wallace, Operator,' he said. When connected with

42

the head of the agricultural department, he said breathlessly, 'I am on a farm here in North Dakota and have just been confronted with a mean-looking creature. He has a hump on his back, he is a bit ragged behind, he has two short horns and a grey goatee. What do I do with him?'

" 'For goodness sake,' echoed the voice from Washington. 'Don't shoot him! He is the farmer!' "

On this note, the farmers broke into laughter and headed for home.

Loans to China and Russia

By mid-September of 1933 the AAA announced its intentions of subsidizing the exports of 35 million bushels of wheat at a probable loss of $7 million. Quantities of cotton and wheat had already been exported to the Chinese and Russians by advancing loans to China and the Soviet Union.

By the end of 1933 the Bureau of Agriculture Economics claimed that farm income had increased $1,213 million over 1932. While this looked like a substantial improvement, the figures were somewhat misleading as the cost of living had already begun to rise and offset a portion of this gain.

30 Percent of the Nation Unemployed

With 30 percent of the nation unemployed, Roosevelt turned his attention to programs that would provide jobs.

The president had only been in office about three weeks when he declared his intention to recruit

250,000 men to work in the forests before summer. The idea was strictly his own. He had expressed these thoughts in conversation long before the depression. When he first mentioned it in public in Chicago, the idea had evoked derision from many quarters. Some of the listeners referred to his suggestion as "Roosevelt's brainstorm."

One Dollar a Day

Organized labor at once cried out against the conscription of labor that proposed a wage scale of $30 monthly.

As enrollment in the forest service was to be voluntary, the protest against conscription made little headway.

When the CCC bill was passed, the Civilian Conservation Corps became an important program in the days of the New Deal.

When one added to the wage of $30 a month the sundry benefits of housing, medical attention, food and toilet kits, the worker actually received approximately $2.00 per day.[40]

On April 25 the first forest camp was established near Luray, Virginia. In order to accomplish the president's goals it was necessary to enlist the cooperation of the Departments of War, Interior, Agriculture and Labor, and corresponding portions of the governments of forty-eight states. The Labor Department took charge of enrolling the workers. The army transported them to conditioning camps and then on to the forest camps. The army remained responsible for feeding, housing and disciplining the corps. During the working hours which were to be forty hours a week, the Department of Agriculture was in charge of the men.

1451 Camps Were Established in Forty-Seven States

To the amazement of many, the mobilization of workers of the Civilian Conservation Corps and their movements into the forests were completed more rapidly than the same number of troops had been mobilized after entry into World War II. One thousand, four hundred fifty-one camps were situated in forty-seven states. By August 1, the president saw his order fulfilled. There were 240,000 young unmarried men and 30,000 war veterans working in the forest camps.[41]

Among the projects to which the men were assigned were the construction of 50,000 miles of truck and horse trails and 12,000 miles of telephone lines to join forest lookouts and many other duties such as thinning the fire control areas, etc.

Records revealed that the majority of the young men employed in the forest camps allotted from two-thirds to three-quarters of their cash income to their dependents back home. The $90,000 a day food bill also put money back into circulation, and the total program undoubtedly enabled as many as a million to be struck from the relief rolls.

The Works Progress Administration
Another New Deal program to assist the unemployed

was the Works Progress Administration (WPA). This program was designed to give employment to the older married men. I visited one of the WPA projects in Eastern Montana where 10,000 men were building the Fort Peck Dam, then considered to be the largest earthen dam in the world.

While most men were grateful for any type of employment that enabled them to provide food and shelter for their families, there was still a contrast between the spirit of the workers on such government projects to the enthusiasm of the self-employed in normal times.

I listened to men in leisure hours joking about the type of WPA workers who were seen on the job. One man, with a touch of humor, said that when one of the workers died the doctor had to examine forty men before he discovered the corpse.

It was easier, however, for the president to enforce his new rules on the farmers and laborers than on the Eastern bankers and corporate heads of the business world. Undaunted, nonetheless, he turned his power in their direction as well.

A Wartime Program

Roosevelt treated the challenge of depression the same as if the nation was being invaded by a foreign power. In a move known as the National Industrial Recovery Act, the president set up a plan for government "partnership" with industry. While the nation was still floundering in the depths of depression, Mr. Roosevelt saw his National Industrial Recovery Act rushed through Congress as an emergency measure. In retrospect, some said the NRA had all the "trappings" of cooperation between government and industry, but the fact was that power was conferred on the president that actually caused leaders of industry to gasp.

Every employer had to comply with maximum hours, minimum wages and other working conditions approved by the president. Employers and employees had first chance to reach agreements. But if they failed, or if the president did not approve their agreements, he could impose one of his own. The president could cancel or modify any arrangements at any time. He could delegate his authority to any person he chose. Critics of the program commonly talked of the new "dictatorship."

General Johnson Heads the NRA

The president selected General Hugh Johnson to head the National Industrial Recovery Act. Johnson in turn chose Charles F. Horner, an organizer of the wartime Liberty Loan drives, to assist him in laying plans for a nationwide campaign. Men said the general tore into his work as though it was a war that had to be won in thirty days.

On July 24, 1933, the president appealed for cooperation in the NRA. Three days after his broadcasted appeal the postmen delivered five million copies of the president's Re-Employment Agreement to employers throughout the country. The postmen were instructed to give them to everyone on their routes who employed more than two people, except for professional men and farmers.

Under the Blue Eagle

The emblem of the NRA was the blue eagle. Soon this emblem was seen in connection with 90 percent of the nation's industry. Under the NRA, white-collar workers were to receive a minimum wage of twelve dollars to fifteen dollars a week. For factory workers there was to be a minimum wage of forty cents an hour and a thirty-five-hour week with only few exceptions. The main objective was to bring the big basic industries with a large number of employees under codes as rapidly as possible.

Oil, Coal and Steel Industries Balked

The automobile industry expressed its concern over unionization. Oil and steel also were expressing their discontent with the sweeping measures of the NRA. In describing these critical days Ernest Lindley wrote,

Mr. Roosevelt in a whirlwind week put direct pressure from the White House behind the NRA. He authorized General Johnson to impose a code on the three wrangling groups in the oil industry. He amended the final draft of the code himself and announced that he would head the enforcing agency to be set up. The general strode into the room where three hundred oil men patiently waited. He spent a total of three minutes telling them that they had until ten o'clock the next day to register their protests before the code was sent to the president for signature.

"We will now pass copies of the code," he announced brusquely. "The meeting is adjourned."

Oil executives saw the stack of copies of the code and stampeded toward it.

"Please sit down!" shouted Johnson. "Sit down or I'll stop immediately!"

The leaders of the oil industry slunk back to their chairs. Johnson left the copies with his secretary and donning his hat, walked from the room.[42]

The general public across the nation supported Roosevelt. They mistrusted the leaders of big business and especially those of the oil industry. They were aware of the efforts that had been made to curb production and distribution. Roosevelt did not hesitate to challenge the leaders of the oil industry nor did he shrink from moving against Tammany Hall and the leading bankers of the Eastern Establishment.

The Holy Citadel of the Financial World

In describing Mr. Roosevelt's investigation of the great private banking houses, Ernest Lindley said,

At the president's suggestion, the Senate Banking and Currency Committee's inquisitorial nose was temporarily turned from the commercial banks and toward the great private banking houses. With a new grant of power, Ferdinand Pecora, the committee's counsel, began to probe into the holy citadel of the financial world of J.P. Morgan and Co. and the lesser private houses such as Kuhn, Loeb and Co. and Dillon, Read & Co.

As Mr. Roosevelt began his conversations on war debts and other international problems the House of Morgan was the chief fountain of propaganda for war debt cancellation and other items of international bankers' solution of depression. The Morgan firm had been for years a powerful and at times a controlling influence in American policy at home and abroad. If the United States had an invisible government, the House of Morgan held the chief portfolio. For the first time in twenty years. . . since the Pujo money trust investigation . . . a Morgan was put on the witness stand and Wall Street's sanctum opened to the public view. For a time the Morgan hearing blanketed the main performance of the president and Congress.

As in the Mitchell hearings, the sharpest public reaction was to the income tax disclosures. The public learned that the twenty partners in the firm had paid no taxes for 1931 and 1932 and only a trifling amount in the aggregate in 1930, thanks to the capital gains and losses provisions of the income tax law. The extraordinary methods by which three of the partners had legally avoided paying income taxes could only sharpen the ordinary taxpayer's amazement at the ingenuity of the big financiers and their legal talent.

There was an imposing list of politicians, financiers, publishers, industrialists, and other prominent friends of the firm who were invited in on the ground floor of Morgan stock issues. The list showed 167 directorships held by Morgan partners. A grand array of great industrial concerns kept deposits with the Morgan firm.[43]

The building of the Morgan Railroad and the utility empires, the staggering profits of the boom years, these and many other revelations confirmed the popular estimate of the House of Morgan as a sinister and mighty power.[44]

Driving the Money-Changers From the Temple

In his inaugural address on March 4, 1933, Franklin Roosevelt lashed out at those whom he described as "The Money-Changers" and in strong language declared he would drive them from the temple.

He was well aware of the profits that had been made by certain tycoons in the business world, when the stock market was falling and millions of ordinary people were having their entire life's savings swept aside.

One who came under criticism at that time was Albert H. Wiggin who had served as president, chairman of the board, and chairman of the governing board of Chase National Bank.

According to the Stock Exchange Practices Report, Albert Wiggin received $275,000 compensation in 1929 as head of Chase. At the same time he was shown to be director of fifty-nine utility, industrial, insurance, and other corporations from whom he received a handsome salary. Armour and Company, for example, paid him $40,000 to be a member of the finance committee. He received $20,000 from the Brooklyn-Manhattan Transit Corporation; and at least seven other firms paid him from two to five thousand dollars annually.

The most breathtaking operation of Mr. Wiggin, however, was his handling of Chase stock at the time of the crash. Between September 23 and November 4, Mr. Wiggin sold short 42,506 shares of Chase stock. The timing was perfect, and as the stock market fell, reports revealed that the profit on that stock netted the Shermar Corporation, with which Mr. Wiggin had his connection, over four million dollars.[45]

In the dark days immediately following the crash of the market in 1929, John D. Rockefeller announced from his home in Pocantico Hills.

Believing that the fundamental conditions of the country are sound . . . my son and I for some days have been purchasing sound common stocks.

In response to this announcement, Eddie Cantor replied sarcastically, "Sure, who else has any money left?"[46]

Who Else Had Any Money Left?

Looking back to October 24, 1929, the first day identified with the crash, over thirteen million shares changed hands. As more people tried to sell, fear turned to panic. Men who had bought on margin received calls from brokers asking for more money to hold their stocks. These calls became more urgent and frequent as stocks continued to fall. Those hoping for profit bought on the lower prices expecting there would be a recovery, but to their dismay they saw many of the stocks fall to a fourth of the purchase price in the ensuing months.

As tensions prevailed at Wall Street, some of the employees did not return home for days. In many offices lights burned both night and day. With the emotions of anger and frustration mounting hourly, Police Commissioner Whalen dispatched a special detail of police to quell any riot that might break out.

Those who saw their life's savings vanish overnight seemed little inclined to riot; there was rather a pall of despair.

As ticker tapes fell far behind, many across the nation waited in painful silence to see if they were still financially solvent or destitute.

As suicides were recorded, some hotel clerks

reputedly asked some of their guests with a touch of satire, "Do you plan to sleep in your room tonight, or jump out of the window?" The crash of the market left investors with a loss of over $70 billion. This would compare on today's market with a loss of approximately $220 billion.

Were the Bankers to Blame?

Men who studied the preliminary events that preceded the crash of 1929, pointed accusing fingers at Benjamin Strong of the Federal Reserve Bank, and the three powerful bankers from Europe—Charles Rist from the Banque France; Hjalmar Schacht from Germany's Reichbank; and Montague Norman, governor of the Bank of England.

The *Wall Street Journal* referred to Montague Norman as "The currency dictator of Europe."[47] Almost all of the former governors of the Bank of England had served terms of two years, a few had served three or even four years. Montague Norman served from 1920 to 1944. Men who knew him said he had little use for governments and feared democracy. He considered both a threat to private banking.

A few months before the Wall Street crash of 1929, Montague Norman and his two banker friends from Europe arrived in New York to persuade Benjamin Strong to lower the rediscount rate to America's commercial banks. The European bankers seemed little concerned about the tragic consequence this could have on America. They were only interested in their own ends.

Some look back with amazement on the willingness of Benjamin Strong of the Federal Reserve to acquiesce to the wishes of the bankers of Europe. He eased America's money supply at the worst possible time.

Congressmen Lindbergh Spoke of the Wall Street Trap

Some congressmen felt the action of the bankers was not one of ignorance. It was believed they were willing to collapse the market.

In his book, *The Federal Reserve Bank*, H.S. Kenan quotes from a speech delivered by Congressman Charles Lindbergh of Minnesota on December 15, 1911:

In 1907 nature responded most beautifully and gave this country the most bountiful crop it had ever had. Other industries were busy too and from a natural standpoint all the conditions were right for a most prosperous year. Instead, a panic entailed enormous losses upon us. . . . Wall Street knew the American people were demanding a remedy against the reoccurrence of such a ridiculous unnatural condition. Most senators and congressmen fell into the Wall Street trap. . . .[48]

Men today still accuse Wall Street insiders.

Conspiracy Is an Ugly Word

One of the most outspoken writers of our time is Richard Ney. His book, *The Wall Street Gang*, published by Praeger Publishers, caused quite a sensation. Ney talks about "the invisible world of the Stock Exchange." He writes, "It is beyond our comprehension that the Exchange insiders, bankers, and billionaires might underhandedly seek to gain control of the country's economic wealth and power."[49]

When Richard Ney referred to the manipulations of Wall Street as "the greatest financial conspiracy in modern times," it did not hinder Senator Lee Metcalf from praising the author and endorsing his writing.

In writing the foreword for Ney's book, Senator Metcalf stated,

> I approach this commentary on Richard Ney's *The Wall Street Gang* with a mixture of pride and trepidation. I am proud that Mr. Ney has chosen to single out in chapter 2 an exposure of some of the activities of the Wall Streeters I have tried to bring to the attention of the American people; I am concerned that perhaps I cannot do justice to a book that is more knowledgeable, more comprehensive, and more informative than anything I have achieved.[50]

Managed News in Favor of Wall Street Insiders?

In his lucid book Richard Ney declares that the Wall

56

Street "Insiders" manipulate the news to their own profit.

His staunch supporter, Senator Lee Metcalf, apparently shared the same conviction and was quick to declare it.

On June 24, 1971, Senator Metcalf asked, "Who owns America?" The senator then entered into the *Congressional Record* the "Secret Nominee List" which gives the corporate code names used by American companies to hide the identity of stockholders from the public.

He began his remarks by saying,

Aftco, Byeco, Cadco, Bebco, Ertco, Fivco, Floco, Forco, Gepco, Nonco, Octco, Oneco, Quinco, Sevco, Sixco, Tenco, Treco, Twoco . . . may sound like a space-age counting system. In reality each is a part of a corporate code. How does one find out that Aftco is really Prudential, and that Kane and Co. is really Chase Manhattan Bank? That Cede and Co. is the Stock Clearing Corporation, which is a wholly owned subsidiary of the New York Stock Exchange? The answer is simple, if you are a select insider.[51]

A Newspaper Is a Private Enterprise, Owing Nothing to the Public

In March, 1963, at hearings before the Antitrust Subcommittee of the Judiciary Committee of the House of Representatives to determine the effects of a continuing decline in newspaper competition, a spokesman for the *Wall Street Journal* said,

> A newspaper is a private enterprise, owing nothing whatever to the public. . . . it is emphatically the property of its owner. . . . Editors, except where they own their own newspapers, take their policy from their employers.[52]

On the fourteenth floor of the stock exchange, the news bureau is the largest single unit in the exchange's Department of Public Information and Press Relations. The men the exchange has gathered represent some of the most brilliant journalists, PR men and news analysts of our day.[53]

In exceedingly strong language, Richard Ney says that Senator Metcalf has revealed Wall Street parasites in the act of gaining title to the nation's corporate empire. The process for doing so shows all the arcane involutions and muscle of the twentieth century's master financial strategists as they fix a bone-crushing grip on the heavyweights of the industrial complex.[54]

History Repeats Itself

If the industrial aristocracy has one fear it is that another cycle of events comparable to the 1930s would produce another president with almost dictatorial power such as was displayed by Franklin Roosevelt. This fear is also expressed by men in government who realize that in a time of national military or financial emergency the nation might inherit a leader less benevolent and sincere than Roosevelt.

4

Dollars in Corrupt Hands

For at least another hundred years, we must pretend to ourselves, and to everyone that fair is foul and foul is fair; for foul is useful and fair is not. (John Maynard Keynes)[55]

One day when studying economics, I noticed that Richard Gill gave John Maynard Keynes a full page picture in his book and this comment,

Keynes was the most influential Western economist in the first half of the twentieth century.

Certainly he was the dominating influence in the financial affairs of Roosevelt. While Keynes offered his philosophies, designed to lead world leaders out of their tunnel of economic necessities into daylight, his promises seemed rather vague.

A Strange Millennium
Keynes talked rather abstractly of a millennium that would be one day established through his

theories of economic control of the world. In his essay, "The Economic Possibilities for our Grandchildren," he implies that this millennium will be established through science and compound interest.

This is not a new thought. Knowing the fearful power of compound interest, it is easy to visualize the world's wealth in the hands of a few. He apparently considered that a few global aristocrats could control and run the world for the betterment of all mankind.

In his essay Keynes wrote,

I see us free, therefore, to return to some of the most sure and certain principles of religion and traditional virtue. . . . We shall once more value ends above means and prefer good to useful. We shall honor those who can teach us to pluck the hours and the day virtuously well, the delightful people who are capable of taking direct enjoyment in things, the lilies of the field, who neither toil nor spin.[56]

In referring to the love of money and the methods used to acquire it, Keynes speaks of a day when things may change. This love of money,

Will be recognized for what it is, a somewhat disgusting morbidity, one of those semi-criminal, semi-pathological propensities, which one hands over with a shudder to those specialists in mental diseases.[57]

While Keynes, like Roosevelt, dreamed of a better world and a golden age built on their formulas, he also, with sadness, conceded the illusiveness of his plans. His millennium seemed still out of reach when he wrote,

> The time for all this is not yet. For at least another hundred years, we must pretend to ourselves, and to everyone that fair is foul, and foul is fair; for foul is useful and fair is not. Avarice and usury and precaution must be our gods a little longer still. For only they can lead us out of the tunnel of economic necessity into daylight.[58]

When reading these comments from Keynes, I asked myself, "Who could lead us to 'economic daylight'?" The younger generation had become rather cynical in its appraisal of both government and big business.

The Whole Structure Signifies Nothing

One day when reading *Global Reach* I paused at the rather unusual paragraph written by Jaques Maisonrouge of IBM. He said,

> If I were asked to describe the current stereotype of the corporation held by the young, I would be compelled to say, A corporation is a business structure whose sole reason for existence is the earning of profits by manufacturing products for as little as possible

and selling them for as much as possible. It does not matter whether the product does good or evil. . . . Go to work for a corporation and you are, through salaries and various fringe benefits, installed in a faceless link in the lengthening chain . . . completing the circle by becoming one more consumer of all that junk. And like all the circles, the whole structure signifies nothing.[59]

A Campaign to Destroy Their Competitors
On the Senate floor in Washington, Senator Russell Long had some hard words of criticism for some of the leading drug manufacturers. He said,

For more than a dozen years, American drug manufacturers have been involved in a world-wide cartel to fix the price of 'wonder drugs.'[60]

The senator drew special attention to Venezuela by saying,

Remember the manufacturer's cost was a cent and a half per pill, as against a price of 51 cents to the consumer. . . . Rather than engage in a price competition, the conspirators have embarked on an extensive campaign to destroy their competitors. . . . Without essential drugs people die. Yet those who need them most— poor people 65 years and older—are those who can least afford them.[61]

ITT Fined $100,000 a Day

When ITT (International Telephone and Telegraph Corporation) was accused of paying millions of dollars in bribes abroad, fines of $100,000 a day were imposed on ITT until subpoenaed documents were surrendered. The reply from ITT called the amount immaterial since it represented two-hundredths of one percent of sales of over $50 billion during the period questioned.[62]

Bribery Becomes a Common Practice

In the cold war of economic competition, bribes have become so common in the business world that readers scarcely notice them. A $300,000 fine imposed by Judge Barrington Parker on Westinghouse did merit a small place in an international newspaper.[63] The fine was levied for giving the Egyptian ministry a bribe of $332,000 for awarding a $30 million contract for a fourth power station.[64]

The Oil Companies Manipulate Prices

After reading Robert Engler's book, *The Oil Brotherhood,* Senator William Proxmire said,

Superlative. . . . Engler understands the oil industry inside and out. This book should be read by not only every member of Congress but by every concerned citizen.[65]

Engler also attracted sufficient interest to merit a comment in the *Washington Post:*

He makes clear how the oil companies manipulate prices, how they take advantage of shortages to raise prices, how they extract the profits and slough off the losses associated with the energy crisis, how they control the pace of the technological development, how they effect demand. The sources of political power are here too: the illegal campaign contributions . . . the massive bribes . . . disturbing, well-written, important.[66]

Engler refers to the oil shortage of 1973 and reminds his readers that by the spring of 1974 there were reports of "surplus" in world crude supplies. Once pump prices increased 50 percent, gasoline stations offered gifts to induce motorists to buy more gasoline at the pump.

Playing With Billions

On May 7, 1979, *Time* magazine devoted its feature story to a report entitled, "Inside the Oil Game." The subtitle read, "Playing with Billions, Shuffling the Taxes, and Gambling on Discoveries."

In listing the increase in profits for 1978 the figures were,

Gulf's profits increased 61%
Texaco's profits increased 81%
Marathon Oil increased 108%
Amerada Hess increased 279%
Standard Oil of Ohio 303%
Continental Oil .... 343%[67]

More Bankruptcies

By Memorial Day, 1979, another wave of crisis swept America with an energy shortage not only affecting the motorists needing gasoline but the truckers on the highways needing diesel fuel. On this weekend alone drivers of thirty-one tractor-trailer rigs declared the escalating price of diesel fuel was the final straw. Don Whitlow of Russelville, Arkansas, for example, said,

> It is just ridiculous. Fuel prices are going up 15 to 20 cents a week in some places. Diesel is up around a dollar a gallon and we are cutting each other's throats. I like the job but there is no way that I can continue like this.

Another said he was six months behind in truck payments because of the increased cost of fuel. He was just trying to make it home to turn over his rig to the finance company.[68]

On May 31, 1979, the headline on the front page of the *Seattle Post Intelligencer* read, "Sabotage Claimed in Oil Price Probe."

This news article quoted Joseph McNeff, an Energy Department lawyer as charging that his and other investigations of price fraud were "sabotaged," by high energy officials. He testified to a joint hearing of the House Energy Subcommittee headed by Rep. John Dingell (D., Mich.), and the Crime Subcommittee chaired by Rep. John Conyers (D., Mich.).[69]

Later a group of congressmen accused the Justice Department and Energy Department of "institutional cover up" and delays in prosecuting oil price frauds, described by some as the biggest criminal conspiracy in U.S. history. Dingell said, "Billions of dollars were bilked from oil buyers and eventually from consumers."[70]

Political Mythology

In contrast to the criticisms of politicians and the public who charged the oil companies with collusion and price-fixing, William E. Simon, former secretary of the treasury and energy czar under Richard Nixon, bitterly denounces those who made such accusations.

In his book, *A Time for Truth,* he writes,

The first problem that I faced, for example, was an explosion of political mythology which denied the very reality of the oil shortage. . . . The voice of ignorance was heard in the land churning out accusations that the oil shortage had been contrived by the oil companies to get higher prices, that thousands of tankers were lingering offshore while prices rose. These charges surged through the network news mechanisms and flooded the country with paranoid suspicions, after which newsmen dashed around, collecting the feedback from the citizens, who repeated the suspicions as fact and fed them over the airwaves.[71]

Faced With an Economic Illiterate

As I continued reading Mr. Simon's *A Time for Truth,* I realized his esteem of the government as a whole was exceedingly low. He stated,

I ignored most of my bureaucracy and worked with only a handful of brilliant, mostly non-Civil Service staff. . . . that is how I ultimately realized the difference between the business-man and the government . . . bureaucracies so often produce nothing but wastepaper, and destroy productive institutions they super-vise.[72]

In describing an interview with Representative Joseph McDade, Mr. Simon said,

I knew that I was faced with an economic illiterate or with a political hypocrisy so great that it stunned me. I was to experience this broken-record "cerebration" over and over again from Congress.[73]

In a continued barrage of sarcasm directed at Congress, the author wrote,

My most vivid experience, of course, came from my participation in Congressional hear-ings which were merely one of Congress' many functions. But they are immensely revealing of the psychology of these planners, of their occasional ineffable silliness, their frequent stony ignorance, and their paralyzing intervention-ist ideology.[74]

Mr. Simon continued by saying,

Sometimes the hearings were almost surrealistically funny. One such was a session before the House Agriculture Committee headed by W.R. "Bob" Poage. The hearing was in fact a madhouse. For one thing, Chairman Poage had a startling high, shrill voice like a mouse's scream. Secondly, throughout my testimony, the Congressmen were all talking to one another with all their microphones open, so they were in effect jamming my voice. They never heard me. In addition, before every Congressman was a cellophane bag of Planter's peanuts. Peanuts are a heavily subsidized product, and Congressmen eat them all the time at agricultural hearings. While I was testifying and they were talking, they were also ripping open their cellophane bags before the mikes and ferocious crackling and chompings were compounding the furor. Running like a crazy counterpoint through the entire racket was the incessant squeaking of Congressman Poage.[75]

"Sad," I said as I closed his book. "Sad that Simon should have such a low esteem of government leaders. Judging from his attitude it would seem he preferred to see the nation in the hands of big business."

Spinning Out of Control

While Mr. Simon was serving under President Richard Nixon I recalled him saying that the food stamp program was "spinning out of control."

In 1970, 6.5 million applied for food stamps. Within a year the number swelled to 10.5 million. By 1974 the number had increased to 19.2 million.

There were indications it could rise to 30 or 40 million. Many of the recipients never used the stamps for food. They discovered they could sell $100 worth of stamps to a black market buyer for eighty dollars who could sell the same to a grocer for ninety dollars who in turn could collect $100 from the government each time he made a ten dollar profit. Some estimated it cost the government $5.00 to give away a one dollar food stamp.

$12,500,000,000.00 of Wastepaper

Speaking of wastepaper, it is interesting to look back on the days when Mr. Simon was energy czar in 1973 when the government spent $12.5 million in the production of 4.8 billion gasoline ration coupons. These were so similar in appearance to the American dollar bill, that the coupons could be placed in the automatic coin changers across the nation, and release the silver coins the same as any dollar bill. When it was reported that the ration coupons were stored for future use, some suggested it was more likely that the appearance of the dollar would be changed rather than the ration coupon.

71

Copper Dollars

The *International Herald Tribune,* on February 23, 1978, gave front page prominence to the picture of the copper dollar that was proposed by the treasury department. The little copper dollar would cost less than three cents to manufacture.

To me this sounded like another repetition of history.

When Greece began to decline, she followed this same pattern. Dines called this the "Grecian disease." It was true also in Rome.

When Rome was in a state of decay Nero added 10 percent alloy to the silver coins. By the time Severus was in power, 40 percent alloy had been added to the silver. Under Gallienus the value of the coin had been debased to the extent it was not even accepted at nominal value. No nation retained power when it became a welfare state.

Evans: "Each Poor Person Could Have $32,000 Cash."

In a 1976 lecture at Hillsdale College, M. Stanton Evans made a disturbing calculation. He observed that there were by official definition 25 million poor people in the United States. And he also noted that between 1965 and 1975 the total expenditure on social welfare programs increased some $209 billion to a staggering total of $286.5 billion.

He said:

If we take those 25 million poor people and

divide them into the $209 billion increase . . . not the whole thing, just the increase . . . we discover that if we had simply taken that money and given it to the poor people we would have given each and every one of them $8,000 a year, which would mean an income to a family of four of approximately $32,000. That is, we could have made every poor person in America a relatively rich person. But we didn't. Those poor people are still out there. What happened to that money? The answer is that some of it did get into the hands of the people who were supposed to get it. But a lot of it didn't. I would say that the majority went to the people who were counseling the poor people to work out their problems.[76]

The 50-Billion-Dollar Rat Hole

On September 18, 1978, *U.S. News & World Report* carried a headline:

FEDERAL WASTE:
THE 50-BILLION-DOLLAR RAT HOLE.

The subtitle read:

"From personal perks to big-league corruption and unbridled spending, new horror stories unfolded on the use of taxpayers' money by the bureaucrats."[77]

73

Periodicals carried such comments as:

Fraud alone costs taxpapers as much as $25
billion a year, authorities estimate.[78]

For a number of years the public ire has risen over
such financial commitments on the part of the
government as the $35,000 spent for a report on the
mating habits of water bugs.

One incident that merited a front page picture in
the *International Herald Tribune* in Europe was that
of the three-inch long snail darter which had been
discovered in a small section of water which would
have been flooded by the reservoir of the Tellico
Dam.

The Supreme Court ruled that work on the $115
million dam on the Little Tennessee River be
stopped because it threatened the little snail darter.[79]

One-Out-Of-Six on the
Government's $74 Billion Payroll

While men of integrity in the government are
aware of corruption within their ranks they are at a
loss as to how to control a payroll of $74 billion
annually, supporting a sixth of the nation's workers.

It is hard to comprehend a bureaucracy that has
grown so gigantic that it annually spends,

$860,000.00 for paper clips
$1,800,000.00 for rubber bands
$5,800,000.00 for toilet paper

In the city of New York one million people receive welfare. As the number on welfare increased so did the number that abused the program. This was true in other cities as well.

In Charlotte, North Carolina, the press mentioned a young woman who pleaded guilty to collecting $6,759 in fraudulent aid.[80]

This was mild compared to another case in Colorado. This involved an individual who bilked the Department of Welfare of over a quarter of a million dollars, in six years' time.[81]

The government was unable to legislate adequate controls over those like the young thirty-three-year-old widow living in her fashionable home, and driving to the welfare department in a Cadillac to collect a quarter of a million dollars in "welfare" money she was not entitled to receive.

Top-Heavy Government

In Eisenhower's years the government had 100 programs, and by 1976 there were over 1,000.

Federal spending increased 232 percent from 1961 to 1975. It had grown faster than the private economy could support it. In 1960 the government spent $52 billion on welfare programs, and by 1975 it was spending $286 billion.

In 1975 New York City collapsed financially.

Mayor Beame dismissed 5,000 policemen and over 2,000 firemen, and fired nearly 3,000 of the city's 10,000 sanitation workers. In retaliation, the firemen's and policemen's unions published a pamphlet which they distributed to tourists. On the cover was the head of a skeleton and a title, "Welcome to Fear City."

Mayor Beame went to Washington to ask for another one billion dollars in aid from the Federal Government, which was already giving New York $2.3 billion for various programs.

In the *San Jose News* the cartoonist depicted New York as an ocean liner stranded on the rocks of bankruptcy and the Federal Government as a rescue ship wrecked on the same rocks.

David Rockefeller, whose bank held most New York paper, warned financial leaders of the world that the entire international financial system would disintegrate if New York defaulted.[82]

Problem Petro Dollars

Welfare recipients were not New York's only concern. Another problem plaguing the banks of New York was the excess flow of petro-dollars coming from the oil rich nations of the Middle East. When Senator Percy, heading a government committee, sought to investigate the size of the deposits, a report mentioned six banks holding in excess of $11 billion from Middle East and North African governments.[83] A few days following this announcement, the same paper stated,

Arab depositors threaten to withdraw billions of dollars from U.S. banks if their holdings were disclosed by an inquiry into their accounts. . . .[84]

Because a large portion of Arab deposits were in short-term certificates which could allow the depositor to withdraw his deposits on short notice, one banker said with a touch of irony,

These could write a check and the bank would bounce.

In view of this situation, Senator Percy remarked,

One of the great ironies that we have is that the City of New York is on the verge of bankruptcy and to a degree is dependent upon the Arab countries keeping their money in New York.[85]

Worldwide Rationing

While American legislators and oil barons battled over the issues of control of oil and its price, representatives at the twenty-nation International Energy Agency concluded that without drastic improvements there won't be enough oil to allow economies to continue growing, even at their present anemic rates. James Schlesinger warned, "The day of reckoning has been brought forward."

The latest price hike threatens to wipe out the halting signs of world economic recovery.

Representatives from Sweden and Denmark proposed a plan for worldwide rationing. But energy ministers, fearful of encouraging panic hoarding, responded timidly to these proposals.[86]

In watching this contest between the producers and consumers of oil, and between the government leaders and heads of the global corporates, one had to ask, "Who holds the key to man's fate in this hour?"

5

Dollars in the Hands of the Global Aristocracy

The Communists say that they must kill off all
the non-workers to make their system work.
This is not the way of making the world work.
(R. Buckminster Fuller)[87]

As banks became holding companies and joined
in gigantic operations with global corporates,
billions of dollars were flowing through the hands of
fewer and fewer men.

Men of the government concerned for the protection
of the old American systems sought to investigate
the consolidation of financial control in a few hands.

In 1973 Senators Ed Muskie and Lee Metcalf
made an extensive survey which revealed that 324
major corporations were controlled by eight financial
institutions.

It is truly a day for big business in America.

91 percent of the nation's cars are produced by
four companies.

72 percent of the nation's tires are produced by
four companies.

84 percent of the nation's cigarettes are produced by four companies.

70 percent of the nation's soap detergents are produced by four companies.

In the decade of the sixties the larger corporations began to move out into foreign lands at an unprecedented rate. As the giants grew larger, the smaller firms found it more difficult to compete.

Each day hundreds of companies were merging together for survival.

15,000 Mergers in Fifteen Years

If Louis Brandeis in 1914 considered interlocking directorships the root of many evils, he would certainly be concerned today. In one single year, over 1500 domestic firms disappeared through merges. It is estimated that there have been 15,000 mergers in the past fifteen years. Not only did companies merge in the industrial field, but the marriage of industry to banking became the trend of the day, and the financial power that was achieved by such unions was tremendous.

The Merging of Banks and Industry

It was the First National City Bank that took the lead in creating a one-bank holding company. Soon Citicorp and other banking giants followed suit, expanding their interests in the same direction. They did so, they said, because their foreign competitors were doing this.

A weekly statistical release from the Federal

Reserve showed on October 24, 1973, that about half of the money loaned by the New York superbanks is loaned to the global corporations.

"Why not?" I asked. "They are so integrated, in many cases it is like loaning to themselves."

When Wright Patman was serving as head of the Committee for Banking Currency in 1972, he said that America had two governments; one was in Washington and the other was the banks which owned $577 billion in corporate securities and in their own portfolios they had control of another $366 billion in trust funds.[88]

According to Wright Patman's subcommittee research, these banks dramatically increased their stock holdings in each other's banks and the consolidated interlock among their boards.

The Orion Bank

When one considers the banking network worldwide, he finds such names as The Orion Bank, organized by Chase Manhattan. This includes National Westminster in the United Kingdom, the Royal Bank of Canada, Westdeutsch Landesbank Girozentral in Germany, Credito Italiano in Italy, and Niko Securities of Japan.[89]

From October 21 to October 23, David Rockefeller invited bankers, businessmen, politicians, and labor leaders to meet in Tokyo in a multinational planning commission which would become known as the Trilateral Commission.

In reference to David Rockefeller, *American*

Opinion stated,

> He is "one of that little group of men who sit at the hub of the world's wealthiest nation and by their nods give stop and go signs to enterprises from Bonn to Bangkok."[90]

54 Percent of Everything Worth Owning

Judd Polk, a senior economist for the U.S. Chamber of Commerce, calculates that by the turn of the century a few hundred global companies will own productive assets in excess of four trillion dollars. This would represent about 54 percent of everything worth owning for the creation of wealth.[91]

Judd Polk probably based this prediction on the growth of the global corporates since the mid-forties. By 1950, the multinational corporations had invested eight billion dollars in foreign production. By 1960, this figure jumped to $20 billion and by 1970 to $60 billion. ITT was a classic example of worldwide growth. ITT, for example, employs 425,000 workers in seventy countries.

From One Billion Dollars to $7.3 Billion in Ten Years

When Harold Geneen was head of ITT,

> He increased company sales from one billion dollars a year to $7.3 billion in ten years.
> Today ITT parks cars, manages mutual funds, operates hotels, sells life insurance, trains

secretaries, publishes books, dresses hair, etc. Harold Geneen was paid $812,494 in 1971. He had an apartment on Fifth Avenue, New York, a winter house at Key Biscayne, and a summer home at Cape Cod.[92]

Interlocking Directorships

Sir John Hugo J. Loudon is another example of what might be termed a "global aristocrat." Sir John is Chairman of the International Advisory Committee of the Chase Manhattan Bank, N.A., board member of the Chase Manhattan Corporation (which controls Chase Manhattan Bank, N.A.), Chairman of Royal Dutch Petroleum Company and Shell Petroleum Company (The Hague), Director of Shell Petroleum Company, Ltd. and trustee of the Ford Foundation.[93]

Secret Records

With industry and banking united in worldwide interest, currencies are allowed to flow from one country to another in secret. Richard Helms, when serving as the head of the CIA in 1973, told the Senate Foreign Relations Committee that the agency had difficulty in estimating petroleum reserves because the U.S. oil companies were secretive and would not share the information with anyone.[94]

When Senators Ed Muskie and Lee Metcalf sought to identify the leading stockholders in major corporations—and how far ownership is concentrated in the hands of few banks—of the eighteen large oil companies queried, only four gave the information requested.

And speaking of secrecy, the Dow Petrochemical Firm has established its own bank in Switzerland, and it ranks among the top ten. No one will ever know the profits that have been made by the money-changers.

Global Reach

Global Reach, a 500-page book published by Simon and Schuster, was written by Richard Barnet and Ronald Muller. The opening sentence of chapter one reads, "The men who run the global corporations are the first in history with the organization, technology, money and ideology to make a credible try at managing the world as an integrated unit." The reader is told, "The global corporation is the first institution in human history dedicated to the centralized planning on a world scale."[95]

Maisonrouge of IBM is quoted as saying:

The world's political structures are completely obsolete.[96]

Beyond Control

In spite of the millions spent by the government in seeking to control the global corporates, the evidence seemed clear that these were beyond control. The global giants had surpassed the government in the fields of technology and organization. Their leaders were not elected like those in government, and did not have to spend the high percentage of their time in seeking votes from the folks at home.

Their conferences were often conducted in secrecy. The Bilderbergers, who met at regular intervals in various parts of the world, were a classic example of this. Their strategy and organization could be planned by the financial wizards of the day.

Five Sets of Books

Some firms, according to one tax consultant to global corporations we talked with, use five different sets of books in their foreign subsidiaries. Set one is to keep track of the cost of production; Set two is for the local tax collector; Set three is for the Internal Revenue Service; Set four is for worldwide accounting purposes; Set five is for currency transactions.[97]

Jack Anderson, the Washington columnist, told of one company which sold wheat to its wholly owned South American affiliate, which in turn sold it to another affiliate in Geneva, and each of the transactions was made only on paper, with the wheat never leaving the ship. The subsidies and profits, of course, are collected through these transactions.[98]

Back in 1972, Business International Corporation,

a service organization for global corporations, showed that 122 of the top U.S. based, multinational corporations had a higher rate of profit from abroad than from domestic operations.

A Dollar a Day, Seven Days a Week

It is naturally a great temptation to American manufacturers to produce goods, for example, in an area like Hong Kong or Korea, where wages are one-tenth of what they are in America.

One magazine wrote, "The brain of ITT is in New York but the body is international."[99]

One can visit Hong Kong and find such companies as Motorola, Texas Instruments, and Fairchild Camera. In Taiwan, he could see watch-makers like Timex and Bulova. Rollei estimates 60 percent of the cost of making their cameras in Germany goes to wages so they moved some of their operation to Singapore where the wage scale is one-sixth that of Germany.

Speaking of unions—in Taiwan, Timex and Bulova may share a union-free labor pool with companies like RCA, Admiral or Zenith.[100]

When the U.S. Department of Commerce made a survey of current business in October, 1973, they estimated that the largest U.S.-based global firms, such as Ford, Chrysler, ITT, Kodak, Procter and Gamble, in 1966, employed 3,324,321 non-Americans, which represented about one-third of their total payrolls. This figure was based on a report only 60 percent complete. Since 1966, the foreign employment has increased appreciably.

When George Meany considered the foreign labor involved in cars, sewing machines, glassware, calculators, cassettes and radios, being produced by American multinational corporations, he estimated the foreign labor force deprived 900,000 Americans of their jobs.[101]

Many Reasons for Choosing Foreign Labor

In spite of union opposition at home, the global corporation leaders do not hesitate to give their reasons for employing foreign laborers. They cite specific instances where strike-ridden plants were closed and moved to areas where union problems did not exist. The profit from cheap labor, of course, goes without saying. The American multinational manufacturers will state that they are driven to using foreign labor in order to compete with their competitors outside of the U.S.A.

Even in Japan, for example, the Japanese Crown Company moved its television productions from Japan to Korea, where the wages in Seoul were only one-fifth what they are in Japan, and likewise the Kasuga Seiki Company chose to manufacture cassettes in Hong Kong where the wages are one-fifth those of Japan.

Jaques Maisonrouge of IBM said, "We are inexorably pushed toward one world in the seventies."[102]

Dependent or Independent?

In past years nations were much more self-sufficient.

But in the 1970s, as Maisonrouge said, we are pushed toward one world.

The Japanese, for example, depend almost totally on resources from outside their nation to survive in their manufacturing of goods. They are dependent on receiving more than 98 percent of their oil from outside of Japan.

The European nations, too, in this machine age, look to the Middle East for 80 percent of their oil. America, with her wealth of resources stored in an expansive land, might well support its people representing less than 6 percent of the world's population, but the contrast between America's position and that of many other nations is great.

But even with all of her abundance, America, like most of the world, must depend on Zambia, Zaire, Chile or Peru for rubber. Four other nations produce 50 percent of the world's rubber, and still another four, 95 percent of the world's tin. South Africa mines 80 percent of the Free World's gold, and so the list goes on.

World Peace Through World Trade

As the heads of the global corporates view the wars that have plagued the past and the failures of present peace efforts in such institutions as the United Nations, they declare that they are better qualified to lead men into an era of peace than the governments of the nations.

When the financial giants of the day point to the men and women of many lands who are dependent on them for employment, to provide the necessities of life, they present an impressive picture.

Nelson Rockefeller wrote,

> I think the answer is some free-world, super-national political being with power to tax.[103]

When David Rockefeller addressed bankers at the Detroit Economic Club, he surprised some of his audience by stating that recent polls showed that the majority of Americans believe that the government is run by a few big-business interests looking out for themselves.[104]

He called for a massive public relations campaign to dispel the dangerous suspicions about the corporate giants that lurk in the minds not yet able to grasp an idea that has come.[105]

Money Power

It is no new discovery to say that money is the power that controls the world. This has been recognized by men for many centuries. Back in 1915, Britain's Chancellor of the Exchequer, Reginald McKenna, said,

> They who control the credit of a nation direct the policy of the government and hold in the hollow of their hands the destiny of the people.[106]

The Council on Foreign Relations

When the financial powers of one like J.P. Morgan and the concentrated wealth of foundations like Rockefeller, Carnegie and Ford back the CFR, you have power. No body in America, outside of Washington, plays a greater part in shaping the destiny of the people than the CFR. When I was asked by a youth what the initials stood for, I asked if he would first give me his opinion. He said it could stand for Carnegie, Ford and Rockefeller. While I laughed at the lad's answer, I also realized that the CFR, standing for Council on Foreign Relations, did not amount to too much until the finances of the big foundations, and the brains of the Round Table, gave it support. Today the 1400-member council exerts such influence on the nation that some refer to it as "The Second State Department."

It Began as a "Think Tank"

With all due respect to the caliber of men who are elected to the House and Senate, one realizes that some of these individuals have not been trained to cope with many of the complex problems of Space Age technology. In one of his speeches in the Midwest, the late President Kennedy said, with a wistful expression, "Wouldn't we all like to return to the days when life was more simple?"

World War II brought many changes in the world; it would never be the same as it had been in prewar days. Military bases all over the world required supply lines and communication links that made the world a single community.

When the Britisher Peter Winterbothom was in Dallas, Texas, discussing the close ties between his nation and ours, he said, "I can only say that it is of such a nature that if you sneeze, we catch cold."

Within the Council on Foreign Relations, the studies are basically what the title implies, a study of "foreign relations." When one understands the supremely important role that high finance plays through influence over political or governmental decisions, it is most natural that the majority in the Council on Foreign Relations should tend toward a "One World" government. Its financial backers are dedicated to that philosophy.

Capital Is a Curious Thing

Dwight D. Eisenhower said,

Capital is a curious thing with perhaps no nationality.[107]

Charles Kindleberger, the well-known economist, said,

The international corporation has no country to which it owes more loyalty than any other.[108]

This attitude is by no means confined to those in America. The British Member of Parliament, Christopher Tugendhat, said,

The "global" interests of the world company are

separate and distinct from every government including its own.[109]

American Bankers in Moscow

With the "money crunch" of the early seventies causing thousands of bankruptcies in the U.S.A., John Wallach, writing in the *San Francisco Examiner* on April 17, 1975, asked a question that should provoke serious thought. He asked, "Why had American bankers, like David Rockefeller, chairman of Chase Manhattan, gone to Moscow to open the first representative office of an American financial institution that Russia had had in fifty years?" Stephen Broening, who had accompanied David Rockefeller to Russia, wrote: "I arrived in Moscow on April Fool's Day, 1973; Chase Manhattan can't cash your check; The Bank of America can't accept your deposit, and Citibank can't help you with your second mortgage . . . but (we) are giving nine-digit credit to the Russians." How could Mr. Brunst of First National City Bank of New York, and Mr. Yankovitch of the Bank of America, explain these Russian loans to those Americans who were crying for loans at home?

Were the loans to the Russians more profitable? Phyllis Schlafely apparently did not think so, for she wrote: "On loans where Americans pay as much as 11 percent, Russians get the money from the American bankers at 6 percent. After putting up only 10 percent, the Russians get loans for almost twice the length of time that is often allowed Americans."[110]

The Red Carpet

When Murray Seeger saw the Russians giving the American bankers the red carpet treatment in Moscow, he wrote about the irony of Communists thus greeting their ideological opposites.

A European reporter who journeyed to Moscow about the time the American bankers were giving large loans to the Russians scratched his head in perplexity and said, "We seem to be sailing in a fog."

15,000 Computers for Russia

For Russia to keep pace with progress, she must have computers. To get them she has to look to Western Europe or America; even the Western Europeans acknowledged that America was responsible for 80 percent of their computer program. After the Soviet computer specialist, Alexander Lerner, dined with Congressman James H. Scheuer (Dem., New York), Mr. Scheuer reported that the Russians intended to purchase upwards of 15,000 computers from America or Western Europe over the coming fifty or sixty months. By March 1, 1976, *Newsweek* estimated that the U.S. was presently using 170,000 computers, while the Russians were using only about 15,000.

Sharing Technology

On a recent visit to Austria, I learned of a little-publicized meeting of the International Institute for Applied Systems Analysis at Schloss Laxenburg, near Vienna. Computer specialists from fourteen nations were there. The meeting was chaired by Kosygin's son-in-law, Jermen Gvishiani, and directed by Dr. Howard Raiffa of Harvard. Again it seemed that America was willing to provide the Russians with technology as well as money.

Had our bankers forgotten the words of V.I. Lenin?

We have not forgotten that war will return. While Capitalism and Socialism live side by side, one or the other will ultimately triumph.[111]

In the summer of 1976 Nelson Rockefeller was aware of the Russian threat and expressed his concern in a speech he delivered in St. Paul's Cathedral in Frankfurt, Germany. The Western world was shocked at his open denunciation of Russia and her aspirations to dominate the entire world.

Western Bankers vs. Communism

When our bankers first went to Moscow, some writers accused them of being Communistic. When I was asked for comment, I likened these meetings in Moscow to a game in which the "masters" played for a common stake, "world control." While both had the same prize in mind, their approaches were far apart. The Western men with the power of money felt that they could win their stake by working peacefully from the "top down." And in contrast, the leaders of the Communist world planned to win through "force" from the "bottom up."

An outspoken head of the government's Banking and Currency Committee, Louis McFadden, said back in 1932 that the international bankers were setting up a system in which:

> Russia was destined to supply the manpower and that America was to supply the financial power to an international superstate—a superstate controlled by international bankers and international industrialists.[112]

Sincere or Sinister?

While much has been said and written about the sinister desires of evil men to gain control of world finance through devious ways, some overlook the fact that many sincere men are convinced that the pooling of resources and technology is the way to save the world from both famine and war.

Buckminster Fuller, who was nominated for the Nobel Peace Prize in 1969, shows how the intellectuals are scientifically responsible for keeping millions alive today through technical means of refrigeration, transportation, irrigation, cultivation, dehydration of foods, etc. In his book, *Utopia or Oblivion*, he writes,

> We are operating at an overall mechanical efficiency of only 4 percent. If we increase the overall mechanical efficiency to only 12 percent we can take care of everybody.[113]

So Buckminster Fuller, totally opposed to the doctrine of Communism still is a "one worlder." He writes,

I am completely convinced, for instance, that all humanity is swiftly tending to discard national identities and instead to become "Worldians . . . nothing less."[114]

I flew some months ago from Brussels to Alaska and found on my arrrival in Anchorage that Buckminster Fuller was also there to fulfill a speaking engagement under different sponsorship. There was no doubt in my mind as to this man's sincere concern for the future of such countries as India, which adds a million new lives to its population monthly. Fuller firmly believed the world population is a problem that can only be resolved by pooling resources and technology.

A World System of Financial Control in Private Hands

One author who describes the goals of financial capitalism is Dr. Carol Quigley. In his book entitled *Tragedy and Hope*, he tells how international bankers aspire to gain world control. He writes:

The powers of financial capitalism had another far-reaching aim, nothing less than to create a world system of financial control in private hands able to dominate the political system of each country and the economy of the world as a whole. This system was to be controlled in a feudalist fashion by the central banks of the world acting in concert, by secret agreement arrived at in frequent private meetings and conferences. The apex was to be the Bank of International Settlements in Basel, Switzerland, a private bank owned and controlled by the world's central banks which were themselves private corporations.[115]

Toward the latter part of his book, Dr. Quigley states,

I know of the operation of this network because I have studied it for 20 years and was permitted for two years in the early 1960s to examine its papers and secret records. I have no aversion to it nor to most of its aims and have for much of my life been close to it and to many of its instruments. . . . In general my chief difference of opinion is that it wishes to remain unknown . . . and I believe its role in history is significant enough to be known.[116]

Impressive Credentials
Dr. Quigley's credentials were most impressive. He served as professor of history at the Foreign Service School in Georgetown University, and formerly taught at Princeton and Harvard. He has done research in the archives of France, Italy and

England, and is the author of *Evolution of Civilizations*. He is a member of the American Association for the Advancement of Science and American Anthropological Association, and the American Economic Association. He has been a lecturer on Russian history at the Industrial College of the Armed Forces since 1951, and on Africa at the Brookings Institution since 1961. He has also lectured at the U.S. Naval Weapons Laboratory, the Foreign Service Institute of the State Department and the Naval College at Norfolk, Virginia.

No Aversion to World Government

The number of intellectuals like Dr. Quigley who viewed the complex problems of the world leaned more and more toward favoring world government. Fear of poison from pollution, famine produced by exploding population, or extermination by atomic weapons influenced such men.

These were discouraged with the efforts of leaders in both the national and international field. In searching for a ray of hope for the future, Quigley wrote *Tragedy and Hope*. R. Buckminster Fuller wrote *Utopia or Oblivion* and suggested the world's problems could be solved if man would only think and act right. But that was the question, "Could he?"

6

War Dollars

**The Great Depression of the thirties never
came to an end. It merely disappeared in the
mobilization of the forties.**
(John Kenneth Galbraith)[117]

When Germany fell in 1918 the Allied victors met
in the mirrored halls of the Palace of Versailles to
decide the terms of peace. Germans were staggered
at the conditions. They were forced to surrender
their overseas colonies. They were ordered to reduce
their army from 800,000 to 100,000 men. They were
barred from the League of Nations. And a reparations bill of $132 billion worth of gold or prewar
marks seemed virtually beyond hope of payment.

In an atmosphere of festive celebration the Allied
leaders left the palace where the floodlights again
were turned on the fountains which played in
beauty. President Wilson said,

The future is now in the lap of the gods.

But in contrast an old French officer shook his head and said sadly,

We are now in a high period that will be followed with a low period . . . then the devil to pay all over the world.

The words of the old Frenchman seemed prophetic. Germany never did pay the astronomical debt demanded by the Treaty of Versailles. Her marks became inflated to the point of being totally worthless.

In my youth I heard some discussion of whether the terms of the treaty destroyed the mark, or whether German leaders destroyed it to avoid payment. In either case, one thing was certain, millions of German people were victims of the collapse of the mark in 1923.

A Spool of Thread Equaled Six Sewing Machines

Looking back at Germany's inflation at that period, one sees unbelievable figures. At the close of 1921, domestic prices were thirty-five times higher than they were in 1913. At the end of 1922, they were 1,475 times greater. And by November of 1923, prices in Germany were 1,422,900,000,000 times their prewar level.

Millions saw their life savings totally wiped out, as the mark degenerated to the lowly rate of a trillion to a dollar.

Elizabeth, an elderly widow, expressed the state of

most in her class, when she said,

> Wives went to factories to pick up their husband's paychecks. Then they raced to the nearest baker or grocer to buy food.

Erhard Schubert of Hamburg, said,

> In 1919, my father sold a piece of land for 80,000 marks, to put aside as a "nest egg" for old age. All he was able to purchase with that money was a woolen sweater.

Elizabeth Kaatz, who served in a Berlin bank during those days of extreme inflation, said,

> People were bringing their money to the bank in cardboard boxes and laundry baskets. . . . We no longer counted the money; we merely put it on the scales and weighed it. When my father lost his money through inflation, I saw him cry for the first time. He used the bank notes still in his possession to paper the walls of the home.

A spool of thread cost more in those days than six new sewing machines had cost only months before. Those who owed mortgages were able to pay them legally with near-worthless marks. Many of Germany's middle class were financially ruined in those dark days. All of this had a definite affect on America. She had loaned vast sums of money to her European Allies to use in waging war against Germany.

When it became evident that Germany could not pay her reparations debts in cash and could not pay in goods or services without jeopardizing the market, the European scene became one of chaos and confusion.

Each nation in those days was bent on protecting its own economy behind tariff walls, quota systems and other devices.

In the abnormal pattern of events, it seemed that America's only hope for collecting her loans made to her European Allies was to provide them with further loans, or accepting an unfavorable balance in trade.

Propaganda in Europe also turned against America. Some suggested that America had profited financially from a war in which she had loaned money to European Allies who had paid the higher price of victory.

These suggestions were followed with open denunciation of America for her unwillingness to "cancel" these debts, which they said were not really debts.

In the midst of this turmoil and confusion, the old Allies of Europe were also seized with a fear that Germany might move toward a Communist left, or a militaristic right.

The Nazi Wehrwirtschaft

When the German mark collapsed and Germany

was in financial chaos in 1923, Adolf Hitler made his first bid for power with the famous Munich Beer Hall Putsch.

While he had support from men such as General Eric Ludendorff, military dictator of Germany in World War I, the effort was a failure. Hitler was cast into prison, and while there he wrote his book, *Mein Kampf*. Ten years later, however, Hitler succeeded in forcing President von Hindenburg to make him chancellor. His next move was to combine both offices of president and chancellor and make himself supreme.

Scorning the restrictions of the Treaty of Versailles, Hitler chose to rearm Germany. When asked how this could be done by a nation so economically bankrupt, he contended that this would strengthen rather than weaken Germany's economy. Between 1935 and 1938, credit was expanded by 12 billion deutsche marks, of "Mefo" bills, issued by the Reichbank and guaranteed by the state. These were created to pay armament manufacturers. The Nazis spoke of their "Wehrwirtschaft" or "War Economy." Some of the German economists were worried and political advisors were concerned that the Allies would protest against the violation of the Treaty of Versailles. Britain did issue a White Paper, voicing her protest against Germany's actions, but Hitler persuaded his associates that the Allies would do nothing more than protest.

Prime Minister Chamberlain shuttled back and forth between London and Munich, carrying with him his umbrella and flabby promises that Hitler could be appeased. As Roosevelt watched the Germans move into a war economy, he said,

> The whole European panorama is fundamentally blacker than at any time in your lifetime or mine. . . . The armaments race means bankruptcy or war. . . . There is no possible out from that statement.[118]

Looking back on the broad spectrum of those trying years, it is now obvious that America never experienced a normal recovery from the dark days of the Great Depression. She was propelled into a war economy that was to carry the Western world into another cycle of momentous spending and eventual bankruptcy.

Postwar Germany

When we arrived in Berlin at the close of World War II, the city was in shambles. The heart of Berlin was 90 percent ruins. Twenty years of Nazism had left terrible scars on a people that had produced some of the world's finest composers, artists, inventors and theologians. The fires of faith were still there, smoldering in the ashes of the fallen Third Reich. As homes were to be once more resurrected in the debris of the bombed cities, so the church must also be resurrected anew.

Churches Destroyed

In the city of Essen, only six churches were left

standing where once there had been fifty-seven. Of the fifty churches in Hamburg, only one or two remained undamaged. In Berlin, where Lutherans had been able to point proudly to 187 beautiful churches, not one was left unscarred by bombs.

Faith Destroyed

Nazism was not an accident, it was the evil fruit that came from corrupt roots that had been planted earlier by Germany's materialistic and atheistic philosophers. Some declared their opposition to the faith of the fathers in open defiance, and others, like angels of light, presented arguments in a more subtle fashion.

Hegal, with his dialectical materialism, suggested a union of opposites. With his reasoning based on thesis, antithesis and synthesis he caused men like Count Helmut von Moltke to say, "War is a link in God's order in the world." Others like Immanuel Kant, with *The Critique of Pure Reason* could deify humanity and humanize deity.

Such teachers as these appealed to the German intellect and also to national pride. Each teacher bore his listeners higher to peaks of materialism and nationalism until the teaching of the "Master Race" was most understandable.

Nietzsche, of course, was the strongest proponent of the "Ubermensch" or "Superman." In his work, *Will to Power,* he wrote,

I will teach you the Super Man . . . the Super

Man is the meaning of the earth. Let your will say, the Super Man is the meaning of the earth.[119]

He believed that man by an act of his will could scale the heights. He disdained the thought of God and holiness. He deemed any thought of such as weakness. He wrote,

Once you were apes, and even now, too, man is more ape than ape. You have made your way from worm to man, and much in you is still worm.[120]

Nietzsche declared he would write his opposition to God on walls, wherever he found walls, but when his nation was reduced to rubble, there were few walls left on which to write.

While Nietzsche was blatantly outspoken against God, Freud in a more sophisticated way was equally sarcastic in his scorn for those who prayed. He wrote,

These infantile adults create a heavenly father to replace the earthly father of childhood. Prayer is equally childish . . . religion is the universal obsessional neurosis of humanity.[121]

10,000 Worthless Marks
After reviewing Germany's spiritual need, I

accepted the challenge of raising funds for the building of the Berea Bible Institute and returned to America to fulfill my commitment.

At the close of a rally, a little German lady handed me a note for 10,000 deutsche marks. I glanced at the money and realized it was worthless. The sincere expression on her face told me she really believed she was giving me 10,000 deutsche marks. How could I tell her that it would not even buy so much as a newspaper?

In coming to America to reside with her daughter, she had brought this money with her; it represented much of her life's work and savings.

With her lack of knowledge of the English language, she apparently had not kept in touch with the outside world. So it fell my lot to tell her that the money she wanted to give was of no value. It had taken only one stroke of the legislative pen in the government offices in Bonn to make it worthless. She listened in painful silence as I told her how it happened. Without previous warning it was canceled on a Sunday in June of 1948. Men who retired on Saturday night with enough inflated marks to buy a brick home, awakened on Sunday to learn that the same money would not buy a fur coat.

When I explained this to the one who had saved her marks too long, she asked in a low voice, "Can it happen here in America?"

My silence and the expression on my face were answer enough; she walked slowly away.

The Hardship of German G.I.s

Today in Germany one sees a great contrast between the appearance of the American army now and in the postwar era. The proud men who liberated the world from Hitler and Nazism and remained in Europe as protectors of the Free World now virtually resemble relief victims. Their civilian clothes are poor, their cars are old and their standard of living is far below what it was after the war. In some areas the same Germans who once received American aid now donate articles to American G.I.s.

How Did It Happen?

Naturally, the state of semi-poverty stems from the loss of the value of the dollar; a dollar that would buy more than four marks after the war, buys less than two today.

This coupled with inflation makes the cost of living much higher than the American GI's income can afford. In the German service stations a normal tankful of gasoline costs over $40.00 and other necessities of life affected by inflation average almost double the cost of the same things in the USA.

$1,000 Daily for a Million Years

The 1,352 days of fighting in World War II cost the American taxpayers over $250 million daily. This resulted in a total bill of over $340 billion. If this were paid off at $1,000 a day it would take almost a million years. The truth, of course, was that such a debt would never be paid.

War Bonds

Having had an interest in money from youth, I asked myself during the war years, "How will a government create money sufficient to fight such a war?" The answer was government bonds.

I remember arriving in Los Angeles on a bright, sunny afternoon in January of 1942. Pershing Square in the heart of the city was overflowing with thousands of people. Bands were playing, flags were waving and a parade of Hollywood celebrities vied with one another in an effort to arouse patriotic spectators to step forward and purchase war bonds. There was no possibility that a major war could be fought with weapons purchased on a cash-and-carry basis. Every bond represented a measure of debt. More than 60 percent of the cost of war represented debts that taxpayers would bear until their ever-growing indebtedness would one day be so great there would be a crash. Just when that exact moment would be, perhaps no one could state. But one thing was certain; that moment would come.

The Cost of Maintaining the Peace

While the armistice brought an end to fighting, it did not halt the arms race that continued on in the cold war. America, in time of peace, continued to spend almost as much on arms and armies as she did in time of war.

America kept 325,000 fighting men in Europe and spent her worldwide defense budget of $100 billion annually. Germany, in contrast, not permitted under the terms of the armistice to build a comparable system of defense, spent only 15 percent as much as America. So Germans grew richer by manufacturing merchandise for sale.

War Costs and Inflation

The deeper America sank in debt, the higher rose the rate of inflation.

Mr. Anderson, a former secretary of the U.S. Treasury, explained in a New York luncheon how government debt increases the money supply of the nation and causes inflation.

> As Secretary of the Treasury I might call up the bank and say, "Will you loan me $100 million if I send you a note to that effect?" The banker would probably say, "I will." By so doing we have merely created that much money. . . . When I finish writing checks for the $100 million, this would mean that I have simply added that much money to the money supply. Certainly this approaches the same degree of monetization as if I had called down to the Bureau of Engraving and Printing and said, "Please print me up $100 million in green backs which I can pay tomorrow."[122]

Eurodollars

The cost of sustaining hundreds of thousands of

men with their families in Europe naturally caused dollars to flow in that direction, but there were also additional causes affecting the beleaguered dollar.

After the dollar was deliberately devalued in 1971, dollars began to swell in Europe at a phenomenal rate. Men, fearing further devaluation, were eager to exchange dollars for stronger European currencies.

In 1971, it was estimated that there were $75 billion in Europe. By 1974, this had increased to $174 billion. Three years later it was estimated that there were $275 billion. Today estimates run as high as $500 billion.

The Beast That Got out of Control

The devalued dollar so upset the equilibrium of the money market of Europe that currencies were traded in a frenzied manner. When the crisis started to break in 1971, over a billion U.S. dollars were exchanged for German deutsche marks in thirty-five minutes.

Seven years after the first devaluation of the dollar, the irrational trading of currencies in Europe continued. *Time* mentioned Andre Levy in Lausanne, Switzerland, whose firm, Tradition, S.A., reputedly traded a half billion dollars daily. When asked concerning this report he said that it was only a rumor. "The truth is," he stated, "it is more than a billion daily."[123]

In speaking of Eurodollars, Representative Henry Ruess, one of the best informed congressmen in Washington, referred to the Eurodollars as, "the international animal that escaped control."

It seemed inconceivable that the mighty dollar could lose 40 percent of its value in its exchange rate for the Swiss franc in a single year but such was the case.

Economists searched in vain for solutions. And what were the suggested solutions? In March, 1978, the Germans offered to lend America two billion marks to buy back some of these excess dollars.[124]

If the United States accepted Germany's offer and borrowed the two billion marks to buy back one billion dollars, there would still be 499 billion Eurodollars remaining on the continent.

In Brussels it was suggested that America borrow $10 billion in European currencies to buy back from Europe some of the unwanted dollars. But even this would only be a 2 percent solution to a 100 percent problem.

Back in 1968 when $10 billion was created in paper gold, men said it would not be a cure; it spelled only temporary relief, merely "breaking the fall."

For a number of years, men with foresight have seen the world situation moving toward a major change. This transition period will in all probability bring some convulsive and violent actions. Back in 1973, a writer in the *New York Times* observed that the threat of a worldwide financial crisis had intensified. The article revealed that officials of some foreign governments felt it was already here and that it could become more severe than the Great Depression of the 1930s.[125]

Gerald Kramer of Chase Manhattan Bank declared the Eurodollars were, "Outside anyone's control."

The B.I.S.

The one institution that is committed to this problem more than any other is the Bank of International Settlements in Basel, known as the B.I.S. Sometimes in Basel one has the feeling he is at the pulse center of the world, especially when he realizes that the banks of America, Japan, Germany, France, Belgium, England and Italy are tied into the B.I.S.

The control measures suggested in some of the international conferences seemed to deepen the problem and leave the issue unanswered. In reviewing some of the suggested formulas for correction of this chaos, Germany's Norbert Walter said,

In the darkest scenario, such measures could trigger a chain reaction that would undermine trade and set off a global recession or something worse.

Looking Back at Postwar Generosity

In the strange pattern of postwar planning, America gave special attention to rebuilding Germany. Russia naturally scorned the thought of assisting those who had been considered enemies.

On June 5, 1947, George Marshall, President

Harry Truman's secretary of state, delivered the commencement address at Harvard. From this time on, the Marshall Plan became the chief topic of America's financial reply to the need of Europe. In four years, America poured $13 billion into rebuilding Western Europe. This, in today's values, would be equal to $72 billion.[126]

Berlin, deep inside the Russian controlled territory of East Germany, became the nerve center of contest between East and West. Between 1945 and 1961, 3,000,000 Eastern Germans escaped to the West by way of Berlin. On June 24, 1948, Russia blockaded all railways, roadways and waterways, in an effort to drive the Allies from Berlin. The Allies responded to this infamous act with the Berlin Airlift. For eleven months, Allied planes carried supplies to Berlin. At the height of this period, Allied planes, transporting thousands of tons of supplies daily, landed in Berlin's Templehof Airport every forty-five seconds. In a single day, the planes carried to Berlin 12,940 tons of supplies.

On August 13, 1961, the Communists built the barbed wire barricade that was soon replaced with the twenty-six-mile-long concrete wall the Germans called "The Schandmauer" or "Wall of Shame."

There Were Times When Churchill Wept

The recorded conferences at Teheran and Yalta reveal the sorrows of Churchill as he failed to impress Roosevelt about the future threat of Russia. Elliott Roosevelt, who attended sessions with his father, speaks of Churchill:

Whose forebodings of disaster darkened with
every Red Army advance.[127]

Churchill looked with dismay on the decision to
hold back the 9th Army and allow Marshal Zhukov
to move in victoriously on May 2, 1945.
In London, Churchill had seen 750,000 homes
struck by the Nazi rockets. These had killed 6,184
and injured another 17,981.
In vain, Churchill opposed Roosevelt's willingness to allow the Russians to move into the Berlin
area and capture the inventors and producers of the
Nazi rockets and the missile plants. These gave the
Soviets a great thrust forward in the missile and
arms race.

Berlin—A Costly City to Maintain
Over the past thirty years, the aid to Berlin totaled
over $50 billion which represented more than
$25,000 for each person in West Berlin. Half of that
aid, of course, came from Bonn.
President Truman also lamented the plight of
Berlin. Elliott Roosevelt referred to Truman's
attitude toward Russia when he wrote,

Truman saw the situation in looking-glass
terms. He said, "The fundamental design of the
Soviet Union is a world dominated by the will
of the Kremlin. Whether we like it or not, this

makes the United States the principle target of the Kremlin and the enemy that must be destroyed or subverted before the Soviets can achieve their goal."[128]

USSR Bent on World Domination

With the passing of time, the Western world saw Russia accelerate her arms production until it was estimated that from 20 percent to 25 percent of her gross national product was devoted to arms and armies.

A study of the type of weapons being produced by the USSR made it obvious they were designed for more than defense.

In May of 1976, while we were in Europe, Nelson Rockefeller, speaking in St. Paul's Cathedral in Frankfurt, Germany, stated in no uncertain terms that he was sure Russia was bent on world domination.

Roosevelt's World Vision of the U.S. and USSR

If Roosevelt seemingly lacked the foresight to see the present day arms race with Russia, it was because another vision filled his mind and dominated his thinking. It was the dream of a one-world government.

In referring to conversations between Roosevelt and Stalin, Elliott Roosevelt quoted his father as saying to Stalin, "So much depends in the future on how we learn to get along together . . . do you think it is possible for the United States and the USSR to see things in similar ways?"

Stalin replied, "You have come a long way in the United States from your original concept of government and its responsibilities and your original way of life. I think that it is quite possible that we in the USSR, as our resources develop and our people can have an easier way of life, will find ourselves growing nearer to some of your concepts, and you may find yourself accepting some of ours."[129]

A Little Left of Center

Regarding his conversations with Churchill, Elliott Roosevelt quotes his father as saying,

Winston, this is something that you are not able to understand . . . a new period has opened in the world's history and you will have to adjust yourself to it.[130]

Elliott acknowledged the fact that his father's stance took him closer to Stalin than to "dear old Winston," and quotes his father as saying, "I am going down the whole line a little left of center."[131]

"This," he said, "was so for at least a dozen years."

William Simon, former secretary of the treasury, declares that Russian strength had been achieved entirely by the help it received from the West. He writes: "By 1941 the Soviet Union was desperately begging the West for aid against Hitler's armies and the phenomenon known as lend-lease was created.

Between 1941 and 1945, a vast flood of goods was flown and shipped to Russia: raw materials, machinery, tools, complete industrial plants, spare parts, textiles, clothing, canned meat, sugar, flour and fats, as well as purely military supplies. . . . an unending stream of arms, trucks, tanks, aircraft and gasoline. Lend-lease was equal to a third of the prewar level of the Soviet production . . . a gift of at least $11 billion worth of the most advanced technology in the world."

The war over, the Communist dictatorship, protected by private agreements between Roosevelt and "Papa Joe" Stalin plundered the conquered nations. "Russia," writes German historian Werner Keller, "collected loot on an unprecedented scale from Europe and the Far East."

The total in 1938 dollars was 12.17 billion. From Germany alone the Soviets took iron and steel works, chemical plants, shipyards, motor factories, electric power stations, railway networks, armament factories, and the huge underground V-2 works; 41 percent of Germany's industrial equipment, Keller reports was dismantled, packed and transported to Russia.

Additional reparations to Russia totaled as much as the Marshall Plan aid given by the United States to all of Western Europe.[132]

It is virtually impossible to assess the full amount of money American taxpayers have paid out to foreign countries, including Russia, through the years. In referring to a speech made by Senator

Harry F. Byrd to the Senate, Henry J. Taylor wrote: "Senator Byrd calls a spade a spade—and more power to him!"

The occasion was a series of protracted hearings before the Senate Subcommittee on International Finances and Resources, of which Senator Byrd is chairman. These revealed that 113 foreign governments now owe the United States a total exceeding $60 billion.

The appalling $60 billion due from 113 foreign governments is in addition to the incredible billions we have given away.

For example, Britain still owes $6.8 billion, and the French $4.68 billion dating back to the days of World War I.

The Soviet Union owes $2.6 billion. First, the Soviets knocked off nearly $2 billion. The United States agreed. The USSR then offered only $722 million and required that a "most favored nation" trade clause be included. The clause was defeated and the $722 million became $48 million, less than one-fifth of the original debt.

Vietnam and the Dollar

Another war that brought great strain on the American dollar was the extended war in Southeast Asia. To fight this war in Vietnam, taxpayers provided almost $200 million daily.

In his book, *The Destiny of the Dollar,* Paul Einzig tells how the Vietnam War affected the dollar. The author was a man with impressive credentials.

He was born in Transylvania, and educated in the Oriental Academy of Budapest, and the University of Paris, where he gained his doctorate in political and economic sciences. He held various posts on leading London financial newspapers between 1921 and 1956, including long periods as foreign editor and political correspondent of the *Commercial and Financial Chronicle*. He is the author of over fifty books, mainly on foreign exchange and related problems. In chapter five of *The Destiny of the Dollar,* entitled, "The Decline of the Dollar's Supremacy," he writes:

One of the main reasons for the deterioration of the position of the dollar was the war in Vietnam. This aspect of the dollar crisis had all the elements of tragedy. This war proved much more prolonged and more costly than had been expected, and it added very considerably to the one-sided sacrifices made by the United States to fulfill her role as the main defender of the free world.[133]

The Faded Dream of F.D.R.

Apparently Roosevelt felt that firm patience in dealing with the USSR would speed its evolution from tyranny toward a free society.

No one can doubt the honest desire of Franklin Roosevelt to establish a United Nations where the great powers of the world would sit with smaller nations and discuss the world's problems in peace.

I was in San Francisco when the first delegates gathered for the opening sessions of the United Nations. None could criticize the lofty ideals that inspired the writing of the opening lines of the charter, "We the people of the United Nations . . . determined to save the succeeding generations from the scourge of war . . . to live together in peace with one another as good neighbors."

This beautiful document was only 405 days old when the world was shocked with the dropping of the first atom bomb on Hiroshima. Seventeen years after its official opening, Herbert Hoover said on August 10, 1962, "I urged the ratification of the United Nations by the Senate, but now we must realize that the United Nations has failed to give us even a remote hope of lasting peace."

Instead of good neighbors meeting in the interest of peace, it seemed that the delegates who gathered were more prone to denouncing one another in an atmosphere that was anything but peaceful. Ambassador Bush said on October 25, 1971, "Never have I seen such hate."

Regarding the actions of the UN, David Lawrence wrote, "Can any nation be safe in an atmosphere of such irresponsible and emotional action?"[134]

The walls of the General Assembly resounded with the cheers of those who lauded Yassir Arafat when he stepped to the podium with a pistol on his hip. How could they praise a man who said, "We shall never stop until Israel is destroyed. . . . Peace for us means the destruction of Israel and nothing else."[135]

Time magazine quoted UN Ambassador Moynihan as saying about the UN that it could develop into "an empty shell."[136]

And *U.S. News and World Report* also quoted Ambassador Moynihan's reference to the UN as "A theater of the absurd."[137]

Senator Goldwater said, "The UN is a forum far different from the one we envisioned and voted for in 1945."

Senator Jackson said the UN was guilty of political blackmail. Senator Humphrey said that it became like the League of Nations in the 1930s.

They Tried Before

How many times we had driven by the beautiful Ariana Park in Geneva and considered the grand edifice of the League of Nations, built and dedicated on January 10, 1920, nineteen years before the world was engulfed by World War II.

And in similar mood, we had walked in the halls of the Peace Palace in The Hague, Holland. It was built in the name of peace and dedicated on August 28, 1913, only one year before World War I erupted in all of its fury.

Americans Gave Much to the UN

No one could accuse Roosevelt or American associates of not trying to build a center for peace in the UN. The American government loaned 65 million tax-free dollars to launch the program. John D. Rockefeller, Jr., gave $8 million toward the land, and the City of New York gave $26.5 million to prepare the site. Within the first quarter of a century, the expenditures of the UN exceeded $9.2 billion. The records for a single year showed that the American taxpayers paid 31 percent of the annual UN budget.

Ambassador Bush declared the figure to be closer to 40 percent of the overall costs. This seemed quite a contrast to the Soviet payment of only 7 percent. A look at the humanitarian program of UNICEF (The United Nations International Children's Emergency Fund) showed America paying 54 percent compared to the Soviets' 1.47 percent.[138]

A Sad Appraisal

Of all the books I had read on the Roosevelt Administration, none seemed more honest and informative than that written by Elliott Roosevelt and James Brough. Elliott tells how his father viewed the crisis of his day, both in depression and war, why he worked the way he did, and died without seeing his dream fulfilled.

In his book, *Rendezvous with Destiny,* Elliott Roosevelt declares,

Today the United Nations is a body made up of many nations. Unfortunately these nations, many of them, are not represented by men capable of governing for the greatest good of the people. Many more use the United Nations solely to further their own self-serving aims. . . . At this point we are witnessing the disintegration of the world. God did not create man to have him destroy himself by holocaust.[139]

Regarding the arms race, he stated,

A huge proportion of the world's productive capability is today spent in the creation of more and more armaments. The Communist world has endeavored to export its social and ideological formulas to the rest of the world, to help the Soviet Union in establishing a new worldwide empire.[140]

7

The Rothschild Dollars

The Words of the Prophets

And thou shalt come up against my people of
Israel, as a cloud to cover the land; it shall be in
the latter days . . . and I will turn thee back,
and leave but the sixth part of thee . . . and
seven months shall the house of Israel be
burying of them. . . . Behold, it is come, and
it is done saith the Lord God; this is the day
whereof I have spoken. (Ezek. 38:16; 39:2, 12, 8)

Shortly after the United Nations built its headquarters on the banks of the Hudson in New York,
we went there to produce a documentary film. After
speaking with personalities in the halls of the
General Assembly, I stepped out into the early
afternoon sunlight to see my colleague, Colonel
Garr, waving enthusiastically from the opposite side
of the street.

"How does one explain that?" he asked as he
pointed to a marble slab as big as a house on which
words from the prophet Isaiah had been chiseled.

And they shall beat their swords into ploughshares and their spears into pruninghooks:
nation shall not lift up sword against nation,
neither shall they learn war any more (Isa. 2:4).

Gift of the Soviet Union

"Gift of the Soviet Union?" repeated the colonel. "I thought they repudiated the Scriptures."

"They would like the world to believe they will bring peace through their work in the UN," I said. "But in borrowing this beautiful passage from the prophet Isaiah, they omitted the opening words of his statement:

He shall judge among the nations, and shall rebuke many people: and they shall beat their swords into ploughshares.

"He shall judge?" repeated the colonel.

"The Messiah," I answered. Isaiah opens his announcement by saying,

And it shall come to pass in the last days . . . the Lord's house shall be established. (Isa. 2:2)

"I wonder how many believe that?" asked my friend thoughtfully.

"Ben-Gurion apparently did," I answered with a smile. "When he read the words of Isaiah's prophecies he said, 'I believe!'"

The Darkest Hour Before the Dawn

While the world prays for peace and the prophets promise it will come, the prophets also declare in great detail that there will be one climactic struggle in the Middle East before peace dawns.

If Russia with her allies and massive military might should move against Israel how could such a tiny nation survive?

As I meditated on this solemn thought, my mind went back many years to a strange sequence of events that all related to the establishment of the early colonies in Israel. Many of those earliest pioneers had endured much suffering in Russia who in the final act of the age would move against Israel as prophesied by the prophets. "It's an amazing drama," I said, "and no actors on this real stage of life have been more colorful than the Rothschilds, and none have played a more important role in setting the stage for the final act."

The Balfour Declaration

When the famous Balfour Declaration announced the establishment in Palestine of a national home for the Jewish people, it was not delivered to the Chief Rabbi, nor to Chaim Weizmann as the world might have expected, but to Walter Rothschild. It read:

Dear Lord Rothschild,
I have much pleasure in conveying to you, on behalf of his Majesty's Government, the following declaration of sympathy with the Jewish Zionist aspirations which has been submitted to, and approved by, the Cabinet:

"His Majesty's Government views with favor the establishment in Palestine of a national home for Jewish people and will use their best endeavors to facilitate the achievement of this object, it being clearly understood that nothing shall be done which may prejudice the civil and existing religious rights of the existing non-Jewish communities in Palestine, or the rights and political status enjoyed by Jews in any other country."

I should be grateful if you would bring this declaration to the knowledge of the Zionist Federation.

Yours sincerely,
Arthur Balfour[141]

The Rise of the Rothschilds

If it were not so well known and accurately documented, one would declare the story of the Rothschilds could not be true.

Mayer Amschel Rothschild was born in a Frankfurt ghetto that was nothing more than a street twelve feet wide against the city wall. The Judengasse, or Jews' Alley should normally have housed about 150 inhabitants, but by 1760 almost three thousand people had been crammed into the three hundred houses of the ghetto.

When Mayer was ten years of age, he was sent by his parents to a yeshiva, a Jewish religious school near Nuremburg, to study to be a rabbi. After Mayer's parents died of smallpox and Mayer left the yeshiva when only thirteen, he went to Hanover to live with a cousin. Here he obtained a job as an apprentice in the Oppenheimer bank.

In his young manhood he returned to Frankfurt

and married Gutle in 1770. Here, they raised their
ten children in a home that consisted of a sitting
room and three additional rooms. Of these three
rooms, one was occupied by Mayer and Gutle, the
other by the children and the third by a money
exchange bureau which some allude to as the first
Rothschild bank.

It was in this lowly setting that the five famous
sons, Amschel, Salomon, Nathan, Carl and James,
were raised.

Following in their father's footsteps, they chose to
leave the formal institutional training and become
involved in the father's business at an early age.
Before the sons died, it was said they possessed more
riches than the royal families of Europe and lived in
splendor that eclipsed even that of the Medicis.

Rothschild Riches

When Nathan Rothschild arrived in England, he
did not speak one word of English but he did have
10,000 pounds in cash for the working capital and a
promise from his father in Frankfurt, that more was
available if needed.

Years later, Nathan said that during the period
between his arrival in England and the end of the
Napoleonic Wars, he increased his original stake
2,500 times.[142]

During the years of 1812-1814, when Britain was at
war on the continent, she paid out the staggering sum
of 30 million pounds. It was said that over half of this
was handled by Nathan in a manner so efficient that

the British paid him a commission that could have been as much as one million pounds.[143]

In 1809, Nathan had become a naturalized citizen of England and founded his own bank, N.M. Rothschild and Sons.

International Banking Is Born

While Nathan may have been considered the shrewdest of the sons, the records of Amschel, the oldest son in Frankfurt, Salomon in Austria, Carl in Italy and James in France were also spectacular.

The boys had been raised in very close quarters in their early home in Frankfurt and had been taught by their father that the brothers must always stand together. The father, Mayer, would say, "All shall be responsible for the actions of each one."[144]

It seemed apparent that Mayer dreamed of a dynasty and lived to see his dream come true. When the five Rothschild banks were established in Germany, England, Austria, Italy and France, they represented a whole system that was masterminded chiefly by Nathan.

When Nathan passed away, the papers observed:

The death of Nathan Mayer Rothschild is one of the most important events for the city, and perhaps for Europe, which has occurred for a very long time. His financial transactions have pervaded the whole of the continent.[145]

Prince Metternich of Austria said:

The House of Rothschild plays a much bigger role in France than any foreign government, with the possible exception of England.[146]

When the French franc was predicted to fall, the experts were amazed when it did not slide but suddenly righted itself. When the financial pundits sought for an answer, they learned that the French Rothschilds had formed a secret combine with J.P. Morgan of New York, who did not wish to see an economic slump in France that would have also affected America.[147]

While other prominent names were added to Britain's list of merchant banks, the name of Rothschild still carried a special significance. During his lifetime, Nathan Rothschild had played the leading role in establishing the price of gold, and after his decease, experts from the London bullion market continued to meet in Anthony Rothschild's room to solemnly fix the price of gold as Nathan had done before.[148]

While the grandeur of the five famous brothers of the past generation no longer seems so spectacular to the present generation, the Rothschilds still present a formidable power.

On the cover of *Business Week*, four of the Rothschilds are portrayed along with six pages of copy describing their present place in today's world. There is still a certain cloud of mystery wrapped around this amazing family. When Prime Minister Heath of Great Britain announced that Lord Rothschild would head a new agency known as the Central Capability Unit, journalists could not decide which was the most puzzling, the job or the man. The Sunday *Times* wrote,

They all agree, however, that the quadruple burden of his name, his race, his money and his intelligence have made him one of the most complicated personalities in contemporary life.[149]

Thou Shalt Lend to Many Nations, But Thou Shalt Not Borrow

Back in the old house in the Frankfurt ghetto, Mayer and Gutle at the close of the day would gather their children to hear Mayer read from the Talmud. When Nathan was admitted to the British House of Lords, he swore with his hand placed on the Old Testament. We read in *Rothschilds: Family of Fortune*,

The prince was impressed with the family's pride in their Jewish ancestry and religion; but, of course, this was true of all Rothschilds everywhere.[150]

How many times had the Rothschilds, in reading the writings of Moses, pondered the words:

Thou shalt lend unto many nations, but thou shalt not borrow. (Deut. 15:6)

If ever those words were fulfilled in a single family, it was with the Rothschilds. One would be impressed with a list of only a few of the nations that came knocking on their doors for loans:

The Prussian Director of the Treasury declared Nathan Rothschild to have an incredible influence upon all the financial affairs in London. "It is widely stated," he said, "that he regulates the rate of exchange in the city. His power as a banker is enormous."[151]

As a result of the Prussian director's assessment of Nathan, he was asked to raise a loan for the Prussian government for five million pounds. Following this, there was a loan to the British government for twelve million pounds, 3.5 million for Russia and 1.5 million for Portugal and 3.5 million pounds for Austria.[152]

Kings and rulers were among those who came to the Rothschilds for money. In France, Charles X did not hesitate to ask aid from James de Rothschild. In Italy, Carl Rothschild loaned money to the Pope.

In 1839 the United States received a massive loan from the Rothschilds. During the forty-three years that Lionel Rothschild was head of the British Rothschild bank, over a billion pounds were raised for foreign lands. Loans were given to Prussia, Russia,

Portugal, Greece, Holland, Belgium, France, Hungary, Egypt, Turkey, Brazil and New Zealand.[153]

When the Egyptian Government decided to sell 176,000 shares of stock in the Suez Canal, Prime Minister Disraeli told Baron Rothschild they needed four million pounds. "What is your security?" the Baron asked.

"The British Government," replied Disraeli.

"You shall have it," replied the Baron.[154]

The Secret of Rothschild Success

While the Rothschilds experienced opposition and hardships through the years, it was often said, "No matter which ill wind seemed to blow, it blew only good fortune to the family known as 'Rothschilds, Family of Fortune.' "

When the Titanic was launched and the eyes of the world were upon this remarkable ship, men were amazed that the Rothschild firm, the Alliance Assurance Company, refused to insure it. Some thought Lord Rothschild was losing his courage or his eye for business to turn down such an opportunity. Would not the premium be enormous, and the risk negligible? When, however, the ship sank on her maiden voyage in April of 1912, men once again marveled at the decision of Lord Rothschild. Some called it luck; others, good fortune.

As I studied the history of the family in its ascent to power and glory from its lowly beginning in the hardships of the German ghetto, I wondered if it was only natural wisdom, aided by good fortune through the years, or was there something more?

He Giveth Thee Power to Get Wealth

Long ago, Moses warned:

> Beware . . . lest thou say in thine heart, My power and the might of mine hand hath gotten me this wealth. But thou shalt remember the Lord thy God: for it is he that giveth thee power to get wealth. (Deut. 8:17-18)

Mayer Amschel Rothschild was certainly familiar with these covenants to Abraham. A number of his ancestors had been rabbis and he himself was very religious. When Amschel and Gutle procured a house in the overcrowded ghetto, they did not ascribe this good fortune to mere luck, but rather to "the Lord's favor."[155]

Mayer's will opened with the words, "With the help of the Almighty."[156]

While her sons lived in splendor, Gutle, the mother, refused to move from the old house in Frankfurt. When a doctor, thinking he would please her, wished her to live to be a hundred, she replied, "Why should God take me at a hundred when he can have me at eighty-seven?"[157]

Amschel, the eldest of the five sons, was the most religious. For years he prayed for a son. There were times, according to a contemporary, that he actually fainted from the strain of interminable praying.[158]

One of the rooms on Edmond Rothschild's yacht

was reserved for prayer. On each door of the yacht was the *mezuzah*, the little box containing the parchment on which is written:

Hear, O Israel: The Lord our God is one Lord:
And thou shalt love the Lord thy God with all
    thine heart, and with
    all thy soul, and with all thy might.
And these words, which I command thee this day,
    shall be in thine heart:
And thou shalt teach them diligently unto thy
    children, and shalt
    talk of them when thou sittest in thine
    house and when thou walkest by
    the way, and when thou liest down,
    and when thou risest up.
And thou shalt bind them for a sign upon
    thine hand, and they shall be as
    frontlets between thine eyes.
And thou shalt write them upon the posts of thy
    house and on thy gates.
    (Deut. 6:4-9)

If God Prospered the Rothschilds, Why?

When God promised wealth, He gave a reason for such a blessing. He said,

It is he that giveth thee power to get wealth, that he may establish his covenant which he sware unto thy fathers. (Deut. 8:18)

There could be no doubt concerning God's covenant. He said to Abraham:

> I will establish my covenant between me and thee and thy seed after thee in their generations for an everlasting covenant . . . I will give unto thee, and to thy seed after thee, the land . . . all the land of Canaan for an everlasting possession. (Gen. 17:7-8)

The prophets told how Israel would be scattered among the nations and once again gathered to their homeland, as God had sworn in His covenants to their fathers. Isaiah wrote:

> And it shall come to pass in that day, that the Lord shall set His hand again the second time to recover the remnant of his people . . . and he shall set up an ensign for the nations, and shall assemble the outcasts of Israel, and gather together the dispersed of Judah from the four corners of the earth. (Isa. 11:11-12)

Jeremiah, speaking in the first person for the Almighty said,

> I will bring them again into their land that I gave unto their fathers. (Jer. 16:15)

As a mouthpiece for God, Zephaniah wrote:

At that time will I bring you again, even in the time that I gather you: for I will make you a name and a praise among all people of the earth, when I turn back your captivity. (Zeph. 3:20)

While the prophets prophesied that Israel would return to her homeland and peace would finally come to the world when the Messiah ruled from Zion, they also described the sorrows that would be experienced by those who first returned from the lands to which they had been dispersed.

Jeremiah wrote:

Behold, I will bring them from the north country, and gather them from the coasts of the earth, and with them the blind and the lame, the woman with child and her that travaileth with child together: a great company shall return thither.

They shall come with weeping, and with supplications will I lead them. . . . Hear the word of the Lord, O ye nations and declare it in the isles afar off, and say, He that scattered Israel will gather him, and keep him, as a shepherd doth his flock. (Jer. 31:8-10)

When I read these and many other similar prophecies concerning Israel being opened for a national home and the Jews for the first time in two thousand years returning to their homeland, I asked myself, "Did God prosper the Rothschilds to play a leading role in the fulfillment of this divine plan?"

Baron Edmond de Rothschild, Builder of the Jewish Settlement

In 1951, David Ben-Gurion said,

. . . whether throughout the entire period of close on two thousand years which the Jews have spent in exile, is any person to be found who equals or who can compare with the remarkable figure of Baron Edmond de Rothschild, builder of the Jewish settlements in the Homeland.[159]

In her book, *Rothschilds: Family of Fortune*, Virginia Cowles writes:

Edmond continued to pour money into Palestine . . . more than all the rest of the Jews of the world put together.[160]

Baron Edmond de Rothschild acquired his interest in Palestine from his father, James, and from his tutor, Albert Cohen. In those days, the life of a Jew, under the Russian Czar, was more difficult. No Jew could hold an administrative post nor become a lawyer, or own land. No books could be printed in Hebrew and all Jewish schools were closed. No Jew could appeal against any sentence of any court; only a small percentage of Jews were allowed to attend universities. During these difficult years 225,000 destitute Jews left Russia for Western

Europe. When many of these came at a later date to Palestine, it certainly reminded one of the words of Jeremiah who said they would come from their places in the north with weeping.

While prominent Jewish leaders advocated the establishment of a home for these Jews in some of the more acceptable places in the world, Baron Edmond de Rothschild clung passionately to his desire to see them established in their homeland.

In his personal history of Israel, Ben-Gurion writes, concerning Baron Edmond:

> Rothschild was responsible for a far-flung enterprise of settlement and rightly earned the title, "Father of the Yishuv."[161]

Levontin said,

> The great philanthropist gives to the Yishuv not as an act of charity, but as a great Jew who wishes to build up the land of his forefathers.[162]

When he visited Israel in 1899, he pleaded with farmers to employ Jews in their vineyards: "Each man should help his brother: remember, you were once poor yourself; do not forget your brethren and give work only to others."[163]

The settlement at Tel Aviv was a monument to Jewish faith and the Rothschilds' generosity. Each time we have landed in Tel Aviv I have been reminded of the writings of Amos Elon who wrote about its origin:

In 1879 a group of orthodox Jews broke out of
their confines and purchased a strip of swampy
land on the coastal plain. Their settlement was
close to the malaria-infested river, Yarkon,
eight miles from the Mediterranean coast. The
settlers were warned by a Greek doctor in Jaffa
before settling in the swamp. "Over this entire
blue and silent expanse of land, I do not see one
single flying bird," wrote the doctor. The
settlers ignored the warning and named their
settlement "A door of Hope" (Hos. 2:15). This
was the first modern Jewish settlement. Today
it is part of greater metropolitan Tel Aviv.
Edmond de Rothschild (1849-1934) played
perhaps a greater part in helping to finance the
early colonies of Palestine than any other
person. Between 1884 and 1900 he spent an
estimated 1.6 million pounds on purchase of
land and the construction of houses for the
colonists. His total expenditure has been
estimated at 10 million pounds.[164]

After Baron Edmond de Rothschild embraced the
cause of Zionism, he was finally able to say to Chaim
Weizmann,

Without me, Zionism would not have succeeded,
but without Zionism, my work would have
been struck dead.[165]

On his visit to Palestine in 1914, Baron Edmond said, "Soon my son James will come and speak to you in Hebrew."

The great heart not only gave 10 million pounds to establishing his people in their homeland, he also passed on to his son James the same love and generosity he himself had displayed.

When James passed away, his widow wrote a letter which was read by Ben-Gurion to the Knesset. David Ben-Gurion referred to letters of Mrs. James Rothschild which quoted James as saying:

My father began his colonization work in Israel seventy-five years ago. The work which was then begun has continued unto this day.
As I cast my eyes back over our work, I think that I may fairly say that we have adhered to two principles which will bear restating . . . first, that we did our work without regard to political considerations; second, that we endeavoured to give Israel and her people all that we could, without seeking anything in return, neither profits nor gratitude nor anything else. We intend to provide the sum of six million Israeli pounds for the construction of the new Knesset building in Jerusalem. Let the new Knesset building become a symbol in the eyes of all men of the permanence of the State of Israel.
The foundations of the State have been well

and truly laid. I am confident that by the grace of the Almighty, the new chapter of the history of our people which began with the creation of the State will be glorious and enduring.[166]

Israel's Leaders and the Bible

When I concluded reading Ben-Gurion's 846-page history of Israel, I was deeply impressed with his many references to the Scriptures. It seemed most apparent that not only he, but most of the founding fathers were convinced they were returning to their homeland in direct fulfillment of the prophecies made by the ancient prophets like Isaiah and Ezekiel. Ben-Gurion said,

> I know of no other people that was exiled from its land, dispersed among the nations of the world, so hated, persecuted, expelled and slaughtered (in your days and mine alone six million were destroyed by the Nazis), yet did not vanish from history, nor assimilate (although many did), but yearned incessantly to return to its land, and believed in its messianic deliverance for two thousand years.[167]

Ben-Gurion speaks of the many nations that overran Israel. He writes,

> Although there were many conquerors (Egyptians, Assyrians, Babylonians, Persians, Greeks, Romans, Arabs, Seljuks, Crusaders, Mamelukes,

Ottomans and British), this country was never the one and only homeland to any other than the Jews.[168]

Ben-Gurion continually emphasized and expressed his conviction that Palestine had been promised to the Jews and that promise would be fulfilled. Repeatedly he wrote such statements as:

According to Jewish tradition, deeply rooted in Jewish history and the Book of Books, the land of Israel (on both sides of the Jordan) is the land of the Jewish people.[169]

Did the Jews Have Divine Aid in 1948?

When England's Prime Minister Bevin turned the Palestinian problem over to the UN and it was agreed that it should receive recognition, Arab nations marshaled their forces to invade the newborn state of Israel.

In looking back on those precarious moments, David Ben-Gurion wrote,

The ratio between the Jews in this country and the Arabs here in the neighboring states without taking North Africa into consideration, is about 1 to 40. Moreover, the Arabs have the tools of government at their disposal. Six Arab states are members of the UN, while a seventh, Trans-Jordan, is an ally of England, and is receiving a large part of its weapons from the departing British forces. The Jews under attack lack both a government and international recognition, at a time when they are faced by seven independent Arab states: Lebanon, Syria, Trans-Jordan, Iraq, Egypt, Saudi Arabia and Yemen. The Arabs have more or less trained armies. Some have air forces. Egypt also has a navy. This is, in brief, the situation—one that confronts us with a more fateful problem than any we have faced in 1,800 years.[170]

In discussing Israel's army, Ben Gurion writes,

We have still not learned the arts of war. Neither our soldiers nor our commanders have acquired the necessary skills.[171]

While the records reveal that the UN did little to aid in the defense of Jerusalem, the world watched with wonder as the tiny state survived the odds of conflict in 1948, 1967 and 1973.

If Israel had experienced some miraculous aid from the Almighty, was it because she was destined to play an important role in a coming world of peace?

Would There Be World Government in Jerusalem?
How many times I had stood by the wall of the Temple in Jerusalem and listened to Jews pray for the return of their Messiah, and asked myself, "If He should come, what would He do?"

The prophets like Isaiah and Micah said,

In the last days. . . . many nations shall come,
and say, Come . . . to the house of the God of
Jacob; and he will teach us of his ways, and we
will walk in his paths: for the law shall go forth
of Zion and the word of the Lord from Jerusalem. And he shall judge among many people, and
rebuke strong nations afar off. (Mic. 4:1-3)

The Center of the World

If the Messiah should establish a world government,
Jerusalem would be a chosen site in the center of the
world. Here the three great continents of Europe,
Africa and Asia meet. From the day men dug the Suez
Canal, they referred to it as the jugular vein of the
world.

An International City

When the UN General Assembly established a
special committee to investigate the Palestine
problem, the committee included five of the political
and geographical blocs at the UN. The majority
wanted to divide the country into a Jewish State and
an Arab State linked in an economic union, with
Jerusalem remaining as a separate entity under
international control.[172]

Repeatedly in his history of Israel, Ben-Gurion
refers to the desires of the UN to make Jerusalem an
international city. A headline on page 378 reads:
"UN ASSEMBLY VOTES TO
INTERNATIONALIZE JERUSALEM."

In discussing the desire to internationalize the Holy City, he writes,

> The same year that Herzl's body was reinterred in Jerusalem, the Knesset and some Government offices were transferred to the Eternal Capital of Israel, in defiance of the UN General Assembly resolution demanding that the city be placed under the jurisdiction of an independent UN body. On December 10, 1949, the General Assembly, by thirty-eight to fourteen, with seven abstentions, voted to uphold its resolution of November 29, 1947, which called for treating Jerusalem as a separate entity under UN rule.[173]

A Light Unto the Gentiles

While Ben-Gurion expressed his opposition to the thought of Jerusalem being made an "International City," he did close his history by saying,

> In days of old the Prophets of Israel required their nation to be a unique people and a light unto the Gentiles.[174]

"Could it be," I asked myself, "that David Ben-Gurion and other leaders in Israel believed that their Messiah would come and establish world rule in Jerusalem, that through His rule the world would finally know peace?" This indeed was contained in the writings of the prophets that were chiseled in marble and placed at the entrance of the UN. And

Ben-Gurion, referring to the writings of Isaiah said, "I believe!"

When I was in Vancouver, Canada, I read a feature article in the *Vancouver Sun*. It was entitled,
"ZIONISM: THE PASSION FOR A NEW JERUSALEM."
It told about the meaning of the word "Zion"— what it means to the Jews. The article went on to report that the United Nations had condemned the "Zionist vision" as a form of ethnocentrism. Christians and Jews alike repudiated the UN's action.[175]

If a day should come when the law would go forth from Jerusalem, what would that law be like? What would be the nature of such a government?

Conflicting Voices

One day when returning from Israel, I spent several hours in London's Heathrow Airport awaiting my departing flight back to the United States. As hundreds of people representing many lands milled around me in the crowded terminal, my heart was back in Israel. What history! What drama! What a story of triumph and tragedy! What an influence on the world! Today the eyes of the world were focused on Israel and the Middle East. Men were asking, "What does the future hold for these people and for all mankind?"

In considering Israel's history written in my time, I thought of the words of the Lithuanian-born, Jewish historian, Bernard Berenson, who compared

Jews to peasants scratching a livelihood on the slopes of Mount Etna which once, every fifty years or so, is a scene of destruction. For the moment, like Etna, there seemed to be a time of calm, but when would the volcano erupt with a torrent of fire and lava? Pushing aside my empty teacup, I walked to the bookstore in the terminal and picked up a book bearing the simple title, *The Jew*. It was written by Chaim Bermant. Born in Poland, he had graduated from the Glasgow Rabbinical College and the London School of Economics. He had served as a feature editor for the *Jewish Chronicle* and also contributed to the *Observer*.

When I had finished the first two hundred pages of his book, I glanced at the board announcing our plane's departure time. "Late again," I said with a smile, "rather common at Heathrow the past couple of years." I felt no irritation at the delay. There still were another one hundred twenty pages in Bermant's book, *The Jew*.

I was especially interested in what this educated writer had to say about some of his own people and their involvement in Communism. Nothing in the writer's style suggested he was either apologizing or defending some of his race when he said,

The Russian Revolution was greeted ecstatically by the immigrants, not a few of whom felt moved to dispose of their meagre possessions in America to return to Russia and witness the miracle of socialism at first hand. A large part of the Socialist movement gravitated naturally toward Communism and when the American Communist Party came into being, it could have effectively conducted its business in Yiddish. Growing prosperity on one hand and growing disenchantment on the other led to the continuing exodus of the members but sufficient newcomers were recruited to preserve the Jewish flavor to the party and to leave the impression that there was something inherently Jewish about Communism and communist-type conspiracies.[176]

Chaim Bermant continued by saying,

Others who had been far removed from Socialism in Russia were won over to the movement in America. What there was of the American Socialist Party was largely a phenomenon and between 1910 and 1920 the predominantly Jewish Lower East Side returned a Socialist Congressman, Meyer London, to the House of Representatives for three consecutive terms. The newcomers were warned by American Jewish leaders that their socialism could have harmful repercussions, but their warnings were rejected with contempt by the Yiddish press, and, it would seem, by the Jewish masses.[177]

The overwhelming majority of American Jewry was Russian, the sons and grandsons of the two million Jews who left Russia between 1881 and 1914.

Jews and America

During the 1870s, more than 60,000 East European Jews escaped to the West. Forty thousand of them went to America. In the 1800s, 200,000 went to America. In the 1890s, the figure rose to 300,000. Between 1900 and 1914, some one million, five-hundred thousand Jews left Russia for America.

In recent years the restrictions placed on Jews desiring to emigrate from Russia attracted worldwide interest.

A Scene That Changed

During my youthful years I was aware of the propaganda accusing certain Jews of being Communists. I was also aware that many Americans were ignorant of the unbearable conditions under which Jews were forced to live during the reign of the Russian Czar. For some strange reason, this side of the story was never told. What would it have been like if Amos Elon's book, *Israeli Founders and Sons*, had been distributed at the turn of the twentieth century and men had read,

> It is hard to convey to a modern westerner even a vague notion of the dismal way of life of the people of the Motol, their special trades, their shocking poverty, their strivings and their loneliness.[178]

Supposing they had read at that time of the Pobedonostev-sponsored, anti-Jewish riots and the suggestion that one-third of Jews immigrate, and another third be killed and the remainder converted.

Thousands of Jews who had lived twenty or thirty years in Moscow were suddenly expelled. They were forced to sell their property overnight. Between 1884 and 1894, the number of Jews lacking minimum means of livelihood rose to 27 percent of the Jewish population. Almost 40 percent were living on dole. In 1887, the government inquiry commission stated that 90 percent of Jews are a proletariat of such poverty and destitution as is otherwise impossible to see in all of Russia. Would it not seem natural for Jews under such a system to hope for a government that might improve these sad conditions?

The Tide That Turned

If there had been hope in the hearts of Jews that a Socialist or Communist form of government in Russia would be an improvement over what they had suffered under the Czars, their hopes were short-lived.

When World War II came to a close, they found themselves facing graver threats from the Soviet authorities themselves.

By 1948, Stalin began his ruthless campaign against the Jewish intelligentsia. This became one of the darkest periods of Jewish history in the Soviet. The persecution of Jews under Stalin continued and reached a climax in 1953 with the infamous

Doctor's Plot.

In January of that year, the press in Moscow announced that nine eminent doctors, six of whom were known to be Jewish, had been arrested for conspiring to murder several Soviet leaders.

Solzhenitsyn, in describing this incident, mentioned that Stalin's perverted mind planned to incite riots against the Jews as a result of the Doctor's Plot, and under the pretense of saving the Jews from the angry mobs, he would ship them to concentration camps. He died, however, before his diabolical scheme was consummated.

After Stalin's death, Khrushchev said, concerning Stalin's plan to rid Moscow of Jews, that his charges were ". . . fabricated from beginning to end."[179]

In life, Khruschev may have referred to Stalin as "the wise leader of the people." After his departure, however, he told a convention that Stalin was,

A pathological liar, guilty of mass murder . . . who thought himself God.[180]

If Stalin did not consider himself a god, he at least, according to J. Montgomery Hyde, declared at the Teheran Conference, "Satan is my ally."[181]

According to Stalin's own daughter, Svetlana,

He turned the country into a prison, in which

everyone with a breath of spirit and mind was being extinguished.[182]

Russian Opposition to Israel

During the 1956 Sinai campaign, Russia sent threatening notes demanding an immediate Israeli withdrawal, and finally during the Six Day War, the Russians broke off diplomatic relations altogether, accusing the Jews of precipitating a war of aggression against the Arabs. The Soviet press went so far as to accuse Israel of engaging in Nazi tactics.

In November, 1956, at the time of the Suez crisis when Israel's ships were denied passage in the canal, Soviet Premier Bulganin wrote,

The Government of Israel is criminally and irresponsibly playing with the fate of the world, and with the fate of its own people. It is sowing hatred of the State of Israel among the Eastern peoples, such as but cannot leave its mark on the future of Israel and places in question the very existence of Israel as a State.[183]

Russia's Evil Thought

The prophets of the Bible did not describe Israel's thoughts as evil, but they did tell how Russian leaders would turn their covetous eyes on Israel and the Middle East and, as Ezekiel puts it,

Thus saith the Lord God; It shall also come to pass, that at the same time shall things come into thy mind, and thou shalt think an evil thought.

And thou shalt come up against my people of Israel, as a cloud to cover the land; it shall be in the latter days. (Ezek. 38:10, 16)

Military analysts are in total agreement that the arsenal that Russia is building is for more than defense. Man cannot go on forever building such weapons of destruction. There comes a time when either he uses them or plunges the world into bankruptcy.

8

Bankruptcy or War

**The armaments race means bankruptcy or war
. . . . there is no possible out from that
statement. (Franklin Roosevelt)[184]**

If, back in the 1930s, Franklin Roosevelt, caught
in an arms race with Hitler's Germany, felt that the
inevitable outcome would be bankruptcy or war, he
would today feel more than ever convinced of this
fact, with the present world spending more than a
billion dollars daily on arms and armies.

As history reveals the inseparable ties between
war and finance, the final story of man's last battle
fought in the Middle East will be the most amazing
and awesome page ever written. Only a few years
ago men would have never dreamed of the role the
Arab nations would play in this hour, with their
control of the oil fields which are so vital to the
modern way of life.

Los Angeles Times staff writer, Rudy Abramson,
observed that this is the first time in history that the

world's strongest nations had to depend utterly on small sheikdoms. Abramson reported that the world's economy depends on Arab and Persian Gulf oil.

The Words of the Field Marshal in 1918

When World War I came to a close in 1918, old Field Marshal Foche declared that man's last battle would be fought in the Middle East. Naturally it would be expanded far beyond the geographical boundaries of the area, but it was significant that over six decades ago men felt that this area would be the focal point of man's final struggle.

In my youth I pondered these statements that came from such prominent men as the field marshal, and asked, "Why? Did they have a knowledge of the Bible and the words of the prophets? Did they feel there might be spiritual reasons along with the monetary and geographical?"

One-third of the Bible was prophetic and five-sixths of the prophecies included Israel. Because of this I became interested not only in the message of prophecy but in the future of Israel herself as declared by the prophets.

Israel and America

In February, 1976, while in Belgium, I mingled with Jews who had gathered for a World Conference on Soviet Jewry. The conference ended with a demand that the Kremlin "end the campaign of anti-Semitism" and allow Jews to emigrate to Israel.

As Israel's ties became closer with America, by the same token, the attitude of the men in Moscow became more hostile to both Israel and America. A feature article in a national magazine explained how the Soviet Union is speeding up expansion of its already massive propaganda war against the United States. The writer stated that Russia is presently spending $2 billion annually to spread pro-Communist and anti-U.S. propaganda through its worldwide network.[185]

In March, 1979, the writer, sovietologist Llana Kass. described Moscow's current vehement attack on Zionism and explained the Kremlin's aims. In their propaganda unleashed against Israel, as related in this issue of the *Jerusalem Post*, Russia accuses Israel in the following language:

Zionism, as a rule, does not recognize the vital need for peaceful coexistence. Zionism should be condemned as a reactionary, anti-scientific racist doctrine, as a serious threat to peace and security.[186]

The writer went on to say,

The inescapable conclusion to be drawn from this analysis is that, Moscow perceives Zionism as an immediate, highly dangerous enemy of its own international pursuits.[187]

The cartoon accompanying this article was that of

an Israeli home built like a fortress with a gun coming out of every window, and beneath the picture the Soviet comment, "You can move in as soon as we plant the flowers."

Is Time Running Out in the Mideast?

Former Ambassador to the United Nations, Daniel Moynihan, was quoted in the *International Herald Tribune* as saying that:

> Israel's security is being threatened constantly by the Soviet Union. . . . Israel's legitimacy and its authority as a nation are being systematically destroyed by a campaign led by the Soviet Union. . . .
>
> The notion that the United States has no interest in any other democratic nations is similar to the isolationist feeling that preceded World War II. "Then the debate was settled," Moynihan said, "by Japanese aircraft at Pearl Harbor."[188]

When America removed its fighting forces from Vietnam, many Americans breathed a sigh of relief. But the cold facts were, that in spite of the cessation of actual fighting, the feverish arms race continued.

Each passing hour leading military men viewed with concern the Russian determination to surpass the Western powers with military strength. On May 21, 1979, *Time* magazine featured a report on the balance of power between the USSR and

America.

The Salt II agreement ignored the following imbalance of power that showed Russian superiority in such classifications as:

Uniformed Personnel
U.S.A. . . .2,026,345   U.S.S.R. . . .4,400,000
Tactical Aircraft
U.S.A. . . .5,364   U.S.S.R. . . .8,000
Field Artillery
U.S.A. . . .5,500   U.S.S.R. . . .20,000
Aircraft Carriers
U.S.A. . . .13   U.S.S.R. . . .2
Tanks
U.S.A. . . .12,100   U.S.S.R. . . .50,000
Cruisers, Destroyers, Frigates
U.S.A. . . .161   U.S.S.R. . . .284
Attack Submarines
U.S.A. . . .81   U.S.S.R. . . .195

War Clouds Over the World
On June 12, 1978, *Newsweek,* in discussing the dangers of war, wrote that the "Bible" of Soviet doctrine, *Military Strategy,* is a frightening book for Westerners to read. The 1962 book predicts that the third world war will involve missiles and nuclear weapons. The article reports that Soviet experts predict that entire nations will be wiped off the face of the earth. The Soviets hold to the belief that "attack is the best defense."[189]

In the same issue of *Newsweek,* a chart showed the acceleration of Soviet buildup of arms. Between 1962 and 1978, they increased:

Men under arms from 3.8 million to 4.8 million
Tanks from 35,000 to 43,000
Strategic missiles from 50 to 1,447
Military sales from 600 million to 4 billion
Total military budget from
25 billion to 150 billion[190]

There was scarcely a day in Europe but that the news media did not carry some report sounding alarm. What was true in Europe was also true in England. On May 2, 1978, the *Daily Telegraph* carried a headline,

NATO WATCH ON RUSSIAN ARMADA OFF MURMANSK

Defense correspondent, Hollinworth, wrote,

Russia has mounted a massive naval threat to Nato's northern flank . . . the largest concentration of military might in the world is at Murmansk.[191]

Two weeks after this report appeared in the British paper, the *International Herald Tribune* carried its announcement:

7th ARMY READY FOR COMBAT

In this article, Drew Middleton asks,

How ready is the 7th Army to fight the Russians?[192]

And while Drew discusses the answers he received from the military men, he adds,

No one in the 7th Army underestimates the weight and charter of a Soviet attack.[193]

The day following the article by Drew Middleton, Michael Getler in Brussels wrote an article that filled four columns of the *International Herald Tribune*. It was entitled:

If War in Europe is Imminent
NATO DRAFTS CRISIS PLAN
FOR U.S. BUILDUP[194]

The opening paragraph of this article read,

NATO defense ministers approved a long-range plan to speed the U.S. support to Europe if a war is imminent tripling the number of combat aircraft and doubling the number of troops U.S. Defense Secretary Harold Brown said today.[195]

But John W.R. Taylor of Britain expressed his

concern about the speed in which the next war might break. He wrote,

> A classic worry of many NATO defense planners has been the threat of a Warsaw Pact blitzkrieg across Western Germany's northern plain. Two decades ago, strategists felt that they could count on about 30 days' early warning of an impending attack. Now, claims Taylor, there could be as little as four or five days' warning, hardly enough time for NATO to bring frontline troops into readiness, let alone bring up reinforcements.

Professor Pipes expressed his concern over a statement by the Russian press and added,

> It is high time to start paying heed to Soviet strategic doctrine, lest we end up deterring no one but ourselves.

Professor Pipes continued,

> The threat of a second strike which underpins the mutual deterrence doctrine may prove ineffectual. The side that has suffered the destruction from the bulk of its nuclear forces in a surprise strike may find that it has so little of a deterrent left, and that the enemy has so much, that the cost of striking back would be

exposing its own cities to total destruction by the enemy's third strike.

Soviet Goals of War

Under the title, "The Goals of War," Professor Pipes writes,

In the Soviet view, a nuclear war would be total and go beyond formal defeat of one side by the other: War must not be simply the defeat of the enemy, it must be his destruction. This condition has become the basis of Soviet military strategy.[196]

Cities Destroyed in 17 Minutes

From Stanford University, Professor O.G. (Mike) Villard, Jr., stated,

Americans have totally outdated ideas of what modern war would be like. . . . It is a misconception to think that this country will be able to build up its war effort once World War III begins. The conflict will be settled in less than 30 days.

Professor Villard served fourteen years on the United States Air Force Scientific Advisory Board. As a member of Stanford's radio-science laboratory, he recently received the Meritorious Civilian Service Award, highest honor the U.S. Air Force presents to civilians.[197]

Even more startling than the comments from Professor Villard, is the comment made by a military leader in Washington, that the missiles on Russian submarines could level American cities in seventeen minutes' time.

New Missile, Super, Super Secret

While Russia may boast of more men, tanks and megatonnage in missile-power, technology is now racing forward so fast that today's weapons may be rendered virtually useless by new inventions tomorrow.

A classic example of this was the complex built in Nekoma, South Dakota, in 1974, called "Safeguard." This sophisticated defense center was designed to safeguard America's Minutemen missiles. It cost the taxpayers $5.5 billion to erect. But in less than one year after its completion, Congress voted to deactivate it because new weapons developed by the U.S.S.R. rendered Safeguard obsolete.[198]

When the Congress was locked in debate over the controversial B-1 bomber, a dramatic technological breakthrough on a cruise missile had some impact on the decisions made on the B-1 according to Jack Anderson of Washington. He wrote that the president's security advisor was first informed of the new development by two sophomore congressmen. The representatives had learned about this top secret weapon during a secret briefing given to the House

Armed Services Committee.

The cruise missile, according to Anderson, is a "missile generation ahead" of the Soviets.

When the president's security advisor, Zbigniew Brzezinski, heard about the announcement of the super-secret development, he became furious, columnist Anderson reported.[199]

As the arms race continued and the fate of the future hung in the balance of the superpowers engaged in a war of brains to devise super weapons, the *International Herald Tribune* carried a headline on June 6, 1978, that read,

PENTAGON PUSHING FOR CHEMICAL ARMS.[200]

Another headline on May 27, 1979, read,

FORD SAYS U.S. HAS NEUTRON BOMB MODEL.[201]

Newspapers reported that the U.S. had a primitive model of the neutron bomb. President Ford stated, "If there is an attack in Europe, the President does have a neutron weapon he could use."

Will U.S. or Russia Win Race for "Killer Beam"?

On April 23, 1979, a startling headline appeared in the *U.S. News and World Report* that talked about man-made lightning bolts that could down enemy missiles. In describing it, the writer said that this weapon would be a "blinding column of white light" with a sound of thunder when deployed. It could wipe out incoming missiles. It could be fired from a spaceship to destroy enemy satellites. From navy warships, it could defend against attacking planes, missiles and artillery shells. Enemy pilots could take no evasive action against it.[202]

When Will the Storm Break?

The Chinese Premier said, "The winds are blowing ever stronger, the storm will soon break." As Russia continued to build her military strength to ever-greater proportions, her threats against both Israel and the West became more bold. Serious-minded men who looked anxiously into the future asked, "*When* will World War III come?"

In 1966, the King and Parliament of Sweden established an International Peace Research Committee which would act as an independent organization to study world trends toward peace and war. On the tenth anniversary of its establishment, the committee printed a prediction of atomic war in 1985. This appeared in their publication, "Armaments and Disarmaments in the Nuclear Age."

The *Chicago Tribune* alluded to this prediction in a caption which read:

EXPERTS SEE ATOMIC WAR BY 1985.[203]

Under this headline, the copy stated that thirty-five countries would have the capacity to make atomic weapons by 1985. This makes nuclear war inevitable, the article concluded.[204]

By the early summer of 1979, a book by General Sir John Hackett appeared on the shelves of the bookstores of the West. The title boldly states:

THE THIRD WORLD WAR: AUGUST 20th 1985.

As I turned the pages of the book, their description of World War III overwhelmed me. It read:

Very few of the men now engulfed in the volcanic eruption of ground action on a modern battlefield had ever before been exposed to anything remotely like it. The thunderous clamour, the monstrous explosions, the sheets and floods and fountains of flames and the billowing clouds of thick black smoke around them, the confusion, the bewilderment, the sickening reek of blood and high explosives, the raw uncertainty and, more than anything else, the hideous unmanning noise . . . all combined to produce an almost overpowering urge to panic flight. To men in forward units, the enemy seemed everywhere. The roaring aircraft filled the sky, ripping the earth with raking cannon fire. Their tanks came on in clanging black hoards, spouting flames and thunder. The fighting vehicles of their infantry surged into and between the forward positions of the Allied defense like clattering swarms of fire-breathing dragons. It looked as though nothing could stop the oncoming waves. There seemed no hope, no refuge anywhere.[205]

Almost three hundred pages further into the book, I read Chapter 26 which is entitled, "A Devastating Response,"

A few minutes after the detonation of the nuclear weapon over Birmingham as the huge damage of the blast was being followed by swiftly spreading fire, and as millions in the British Isles reacted in dumb horror to the emergency transmissions on their television screen and radios, the President of the United States was speaking to the Prime Minister. The time was 1035 hours Greenwich Mean Time, 0535 Eastern Standard Time. It was at once agreed that immediate retaliation was necessary, if only to avoid a catastrophic decline in civilian and military morale. The French President was called and gave his instant concurrence. As the other Allies were being informed, instructions were already on their way to two SSBN, one American and one British, to launch two missiles each, targeted on the city of Minsk. The epicenter was to be directly over the middle of the city at 3000 meters. Each submarine reported a trouble-free launch, exactly on time, and the multiple warheads from the missiles tailored exactly to their task, detonated on target in quick succession. The effect was cataclysmic. It was the horror of Birmingham repeated, only many times worse, scarcely mitigated at all by civil defense precautions. There was no TV or radio reporting of the attack. The news spread, nonetheless, like wildfire around the world. Its impact everywhere was enormous but nowhere more than within the Soviet and its satellites.[206]

Russian Defeat

Regarding the length of World War III, the author wrote:

The period of full-scale hostilities between the forces of the Atlantic Alliance and the Warsaw Pact was short. . . . no more in fact, than a few weeks.[207]

The fighting could scarcely have gone on for very long in any case. Neither side could have sustained for more than a few weeks the expenditure of aircraft and of missiles and other stock.[208]

Regarding the weakness of the powers of the Warsaw Pact, the author said that while the Western Allies were vastly outnumbered, they did show in astonishing fashion how far the electronic technology of the West outstripped that of the Eastern Bloc.

The author also spoke of the young Red army officer under the deadening hand of total conformity. And in the field of grand strategy, the Soviet

Union found itself in deep water. It was attempting to handle an almost worldwide problem of war command, with operations proceeding simultaneously from Bodo in Norway to Berbera in Northeast Africa, from the Caribbean to the Caucasus. This was beyond the powers of the centralized system of control on which the regime depended. And regarding the doctrines of Communism, the author wrote,

If the revolutionary genius of Lenin had not harnessed to the advancement of Marxism a huge and backward group of peoples accustomed to absolutism—most of them Asiatic and some still semi-savage—it might have been consigned to the dustheap of history long ago and this particular nightmare might never have occurred at all.[209]

But in considering the various causes for Russian defeat, it seemed that a major cause was that of inner hatred on the part of the people for their rulers that had subjected them to totalitarian control. The writer stated,

The Marxist-Leninist empire, as hated, feared, perhaps as any regime the world has ever seen, collapsed in total ruin.[210]

I was especially impressed with the brief, yet strong, statement made by the writer concerning

America.

North America was undamaged by the Third World War just as it had been by the First and Second.[211]

The Credentials of the Authors

While no human is infallible, and all humans are subject to mistakes, it goes without saying that words are more weighty when spoken by men of authority. General Sir John Hackett is considered by many the foremost soldier-scholar of his time. During World War II, Sir John was decorated three times for gallantry, the last time when he commanded one of the two parachute brigades at Arnhem, in a military career that saw him Deputy Chief of the General Staff and ended with command of the Northern Army Group in NATO as Commander-in-Chief of the British Army of the Rhine. He presently is Visiting Professor in Classics at King's College, London. General Hackett was assisted in writing his book by Air Chief Marshal Sir John Barraclough, Brigadier Kenneth Hunt, Vice Admiral Sir Ian McGeoch and Major General John Strawson.

The Voice of the Prophets From the Bible

While General Sir John Hackett and his notable assistants gave technical reasons to back their prediction of Russia's defeat, the prophets of the Scriptures had much to say on this subject.

9

The Destruction
of Communism

**I will turn thee back, and leave but the sixth
part of thee. (Ezek. 39:2)**

When the prophet Ezekiel made this solemn statement around the time of B.C. 587, he was speaking
for God. He declared that this prediction was not for
his time but for the "latter days."

While the Bible is quick to point out the failures of
Israel, it is equally plain in showing how those who
have opposed Israel have suffered.

Long ago God said to Abraham,

I will bless them that bless thee, and curse him
that curseth thee. (Gen. 12:3)

Ezekiel Foretells Russia's Defeat

In B.C. 587 the prophet Ezekiel made some
amazing prophecies concerning Russia and her
allies. He not only predicted an invasion against

Israel but graphically describes Russia's defeat. He writes,

> In the latter years thou shalt come into the land that is brought back from the sword, and is gathered out of many people, against the mountains of Israel.
>
> Thou shalt ascend and come like a storm, thou shalt be like a cloud to cover the land, thou, and all thy bands, and many people with thee.
>
> And thou shalt come from thy place out of the north parts, thou, and many people with thee. . . . And thou shalt come up against my people of Israel, as a cloud to cover the land; it shall be in the latter days. . . .
>
> And it shall come to pass at the same time . . . saith the Lord God, that my fury shall come up in my face.
>
> And I will turn thee back, and leave but the sixth part of thee. . . .
>
> And seven months shall the house of Israel be burying of them, that they may cleanse the land. (Ezek. 38:8, 9, 15, 16, 18; 39:2, 12)

How Will Russia Be Defeated?

In asking how Russia and her allies could suffer such overwhelming defeat, one answers the question by following the rule of interpretation which advocates a "search of precedent." Oliver Wendell Holmes, the great attorney, said, "A page of history is worth a volume of logic." He would not judge a case without searching for a precedent.

Back in B.C. 896, the children of Moab, Ammon, and Mount Seir all united in an invasion of Israel. And when King Jehoshaphat saw himself so outnumbered with the invaders, he "set himself to seek the Lord, and proclaimed a fast throughout all Judah" (2 Chron. 20:3). And when Jehoshaphat's small army, led by the singers, arrived at the scene of battle,

They looked unto the multitude, and behold they were dead bodies fallen to the earth, and none escaped. (2 Chron. 20:24)

How did it happen? They destroyed themselves by turning on each other.

For the children of Ammon and Moab stood up against the inhabitants of mount Seir, utterly to slay and destroy them: and when they had made an end of the inhabitants of Seir, everyone helped to destroy another. (2 Chron. 20:23)

On April 14, 1976, Andrei Amalrik's picture was displayed on the front page of Europe's *International Herald Tribune,* along with a statement which read,

The work for which he is best known in the West is his long essay entitled, "Will the Soviet

It is a portrait of a grim society whose stagnation exposes it to the prospects of a violent revolution. The Soviet Regime, he guesses, will collapse sometime between 1980 and 1985.

Many men from behind the Iron Curtain have shared with us the discontent and even hatred for the rule of the Kremlin over areas of Hungary, Czechoslovakia and Poland, etc.

Even within the Arab bloc there is a great lack of cohesion.

Fire From the Sky

When the Russian-backed invasion of Israel begins, there will be more than internal problems confronting them. That will be only one element of their defeat. The prophet Ezekiel makes it clear that there will be fire from above. Whether this represents atom power released by Israel, or her allies, I do not know. But the prophet makes it exceedingly plain that it comes as a destruction allowed by the Almighty, who said through His prophet,

In my jealousy and in the fire of my
wrath have I spoken,
Surely in that day there will be a great
shaking in the land of Israel. (Ezek. 38:19)

Regarding the invaders, God says,

I will plead against him with pestilence and with blood; and I will rain upon him, and upon his bands, and upon the many people that are with him, an overflowing rain and great hailstones, fire, and brimstone. (Ezek. 38:22)

There is scarcely a day but the news of the world warns about the coming confrontation that will break in the Middle East. The modern weapons that are now developed can make yesterday's almost obsolete overnight. The potential power of scientific destruction is not only beyond man's comprehension; many of the newer weapons are not even discussed.

Among the new things, however, that are mentioned with limited notoriety, are such things as the anti-tank atomizer. It is a bomb that would explode with such intense heat as to literally atomize an opposing tank—cause it to disintegrate into a puddle of molten metal, or a puff of vapor.[213]

Volumes could be written about what is said concerning war in outer space. This is where the major issues of the next and final war will be settled. In the *International Herald Tribune,* a headline read,

U.S. TO BUILD SATELLITE KILLER IN CASE OF WAR IN SPACE.[214]

Five-Sixths of the Invading Army Destroyed
Whether it is "internal conflict in their own ranks"

or "modern weapons used by Israelis or their Allies," or "divine intervention from the heavens," or "all combined," the prophet Ezekiel is most explicit in speaking on behalf of the Almighty when he writes,

I . . . will cause thee to come up from the north parts, and will bring thee upon the mountains of Israel . . . I will send a fire . . . and leave but the sixth part of thee. (Ezek. 39:2, 6)

When I read that this "killer beam" was compared to both "thunder and lightning" and would sweep the heavens in a time of missile warfare, I immediately thought of the descriptive language used by the prophet John who wrote almost 2,000 years previously concerning the coming Battle of Armageddon.

And he gathered them together into a place called in the Hebrew tongue Armageddon. And there were . . . thunders, and lightnings . . . and the cities of the nations fell . . . and there fell upon men a great hail out of heaven, every stone about the weight of a talent. (Rev. 16:16-21)

Speaking of Great Hail

When Captain Eddy returned from the Marshall Islands and the testing of the hydrogen bomb, I spoke with him in San Diego, California. He told of the concussion of the blast forcing moist air high

180

into the heavens at such speed, that the moisture reaching the sub-zero altitude froze into huge hailstones and descended with force sufficient to dent the armor plate of ships.

And in describing Russia's move against Israel at this period of history, the prophet Ezekiel, who wrote six centuries earlier than John, says,

> I will rain upon him . . . great hailstones, fire, and brimstone. (Ezek. 38:22)

And in the same chapter the prophet adds concerning Israel,

> Then shall they know that I am the Lord their God, which caused them to be led into captivity among the heathen: but I have gathered them unto their own land. . . . Neither will I hide my face any more from them: for I have poured out my spirit upon the house of Israel, saith the Lord God. (Ezek. 39:28-29)

While the prophet Ezekiel portrayed the destruction of Russia and her allies and the survival of Israel, still one brief final chapter of trouble was to be experienced before the world would know global peace.

10

The Devil's Dictator

**And power was given him over all . . .
nations. . . . he maketh fire come down from
heaven. . . . He causeth all both small and
great, rich and poor, free and bond to receive a
mark in their right hand, or in their foreheads:
and that no man might buy or sell save he that
had the mark. (Rev. 13:7, 13, 16, 17)**

When the atomic bomb was dropped on Hiroshima on August 6, 1945, the world realized a power
had been discovered that is capable of destroying
mankind. In the interest of survival, a cry arose from
intellectuals for a world government. Albert Einstein said,

The secret of the bomb should be committed to
a world government, and the U.S.A. should
announce its readiness to give it to a world
government.

In his conversation with Einstein, Raymond
Swing said,

Either we will find a way to establish a world

government or we will perish in a war of the atom.

And Sumner Wells added,

No world government of the character envisaged by Professor Einstein would function unless it possessed power to exercise complete control over the armaments of each country.[215]

A World Constitution

Driven by fear for the future, men worked feverishly on a draft of a world constitution. *Britannica* Encyclopedia in its volume, *Great Ideas for Today,* 1971, described on page 345 a summary of the 4,500 page draft for such a constitution which would have:

> The Chamber of Guardians
> The Supreme Court
> The Grand Council
> The Tribune of the People
> And the President.

While advocates of world government detected the reluctance of many to commit themselves into the hands of such a government, the same advocates said,

Perhaps it will take one more demonstration of destruction of the atom bomb to make people willing to surrender to a world power.

The Cuban Missile Crisis in 1962

In a time of severe crisis, men will always surrender to a power in the name of survival. On a national scope, this was demonstrated most vividly in 1962 when the Cuban Missile crisis threatened the world. One year after the crisis, a writer in *Newsweek* wrote that only one step had remained before "pushing the button."[216]

Knowing that a nuclear war would be fought in a matter of minutes, hours, or at best a few days, Congress immediately took steps to prepare for such.

A series of emergency measures were formulated, to be followed in the event of a full confrontation, and they were signed into law by the late John F. Kennedy. They stand today exactly as they were signed on February 16 and February 27, 1962. Those emergency documents provide that the president should have complete and final dictatorial control, the authority to undertake immediate and decisive action. His excutive orders are to be carried out through the Office of Emergency Planning and they are to be put into effect in any time of increased international tension or economic or financial crisis.

Unlimited Power for the President

These orders are all-inclusive:

Executive Order 10995—take over all communication media.

Executive Order 10997—take over all electric power, petroleum, gas, fuels, and minerals.

Executive Order 10998—take over all food resources and farms.

Executive Order 10999—take over all methods of transportation, highways and seaports.

Executive Order 11000—mobilization of civilians and work forces under governmental supervision.

Executive Order 11001—take over all health, welfare and educational functions.

Executive Order 11002—The Postmaster General, a member of the President's Cabinet, will operate a nationwide registration of all persons.

Executive Order 11003—to take over all airports and aircraft.

Executive Order 11004—take over housing and finance authorities—to relocate communities—to build new housing with public funds—designate areas to be abandoned as unsafe—establish new locations for populations.

Executive Order 11005—take over all railroads, inland waterways, and public storage facilities.

Executive Order 11051—designate responsibilities of Office of Emergency Planning, give authorization to put all other executive orders in effect in times of increased international tension or economic or financial crisis.

Mr. Kennedy did not refuse this offer of power to be given the president in time of crisis. His well-known statement was oft repeated,

If man does not bring an end to war then war will bring an end to mankind.

While still a senator, he had submitted bill 7277, suggesting that atomic weapons be placed in the hands of a world committee with an international head.

As senators continued to view the arms race and the ever-present dangers of war, they also realized the possibility of the nation falling into the hands of a president who would usurp the power as a dictator in their own land.

Danger of a Dictator

In 1973, a senate committee headed by Senators Frank Church and Charles Mathias, Jr. produced a 607-page document which carried this title on the review:

PRESIDENT'S EMERGENCY POWERS
HELD TOO VAST

In reviewing the committee's conclusions, the press announced:

SENATE GROUP FINDS NEAR-
AUTHORITARIAN STATUS HAS BEEN
HELD IN EFFECT SINCE 1933.[217]

The copy that followed reported that emergency rule gives a president the opportunity to seize "near-authoritarian" powers to take over property, organize and control production, institute martial law, etc. The co-chairman of the Senate committee warned that such wholesale granting of authority to the president could lead to a dictatorship.[218]

They Looked at Him as Though He Were the Messiah

As I read the warning from the senate subcommittee, I recalled Hitler's ascent to power in the 1930s. William Shirer, correspondent for Columbia Broadcasting System wrote in his *Berlin Diary:*

I got my first glimpse of Hitler as he drove by the Wurtemberger Hof to his own headquarters at the Deutscher Hof. . . . About 10:00 I got caught in a mob of about 10,000 hysterics who jammed the moat in front of Hitler's hotel shouting, "We want the Führer!"

I was literally shocked at the faces, especially those of the women. When Hitler finally appeared on the balcony for a moment . . . they looked at him as though he were the Messiah.

Hitler's effect on people was not confined to the production of hysteria in crowds. The magic worked equally well on a personal level. Göring, who was probably as close to him as any other German . . . collapsed under the impact of his extraordinary personality.[219]

I never heard Hitler in person, but I did by radio. Later I talked with some of the men who had been in his intelligence department. "It was strange," they said, "the sound waves of a speaker's voice can be measured in keeping with his emotions. Men have been able to make voice prints and tell the degree of the speaker's anger, fear or fervency. But the vibrations of his voice broke all rules and defied normal explanation."

Hermann Rauschning, who was close to Hitler, said,

He wakes up in the night, screaming and in convulsions. He calls for help, and appears to be half-paralyzed. He is seized with panic that makes him tremble until the bed shakes. He utters confused and unintelligible sounds, gasping as if on the point of suffocation. . . . Hitler was standing up in his room, swaying and looking all around him as if he were lost. "It's he, it's he," he groaned; "he's come for me!" His lips were white; he was sweating profusely. Suddenly he uttered a string of meaningless figures, then words and scraps of sentences. It was terrifying. He used strange expressions strung together in bizarre disorder. Then he relapsed again into silence, but his lips still continued to move. He was then given a friction

189

and something to drink. Then suddenly he screamed: "There! There! Over in the corner! He is there!" All the time stamping his feet and shouting. . . .[220]

A man who was intimately associated with Hitler in his early life was Dr. Stein. He was born in Vienna in 1891, the second son of a wealthy and influential Austrian barrister who specialized in international law.

Dr. Stein lectured extensively in Asia Minor and was guest of Kemal Ataturk, Dictator of Turkey. He established his academic reputation in Germany, however, he is best known for his extensive work in medieval history. He came to Britain in the capacity of an economist, accompanying King Leopold of the Belgians on his state visit to London in 1936. In this capacity, he helped frame the famous speech delivered by the Belgian King at Guildhall which first envisaged a European Common Market.[221]

Dr. Stein's description of Hitler would apparently agree with that of Hermann Rauschning. Stein said,

Adolf Hitler stood beside him like a man in a trance, a man over whom some dreadful magic spell had been cast. His face was flushed and his brooding eyes shone with an alien emanation. His whole physiognomy and stance appeared transformed as if some mighty spirit now inhabited his very soul, creating within and around him a kind of evil transfiguration of its own nature and power.

Was he a witness of the incorporation of the spirit of the Anti-Christ in this deluded human soul? he asked himself. Had this tramp from the dosshouse momentarily become the vessel of that spirit which the Bible called "Lucifer"?

The strange transformation which Stein was witnessing in its early beginnings would later be described by others who saw this Luciferic possession take place yet more concretely as Hitler rose step by step to the very pinnacle of power.[222]

Diabolic

As Hitler ascended to his pinnacle of power, his hatred and persecution of the Jews increased accordingly. No truer picture could be described than that which comes from *The Diary of Anne Frank*.

On Saturday, June 20, 1942, she wrote,

Jews must wear a yellow star.
Jews must hand in their bicycles.
Jews are banned from trams and forbidden to drive, are allowed to do their shopping between three and five, in shops only bearing the signs Jew Shops.
Jews must go indoors at 8 and are not allowed to even sit in their own gardens.
They are not allowed to visit cinemas, theaters, or any place of entertainment.

Jews are not allowed to take part in any public sports. Swimming, baths, tennis courts, etc. are all prohibited to them.
Jews may not visit Christians.[223]

November 19, 1942

Dussell has told us a lot about the outside world, which we have missed for so long now. He had very sad news. Countless friends and acquintances have gone to a terrible fate. I often see rows of good innocent people accompanied by crying children walking on and on. . . . No one is spared. . . . Old people, babies, expectant mothers, the sick. . . . I feel wicked sleeping in a warm bed, while my dearest friends have been knocked down or have fallen into a gutter somewhere out in the cold night . . . all because they are Jews.[224]

January 13, 1943

It is terrible outside. Day and night more of these poor miserable people are being dragged off. Families are torn apart, the men, women and children all being separated. Children coming home from school find their parents have disappeared. Women return from shopping to find their homes shut up and their families gone.[225]

On March 22, 1943, Nazis surrounded the village of Khatyn and burned all the inhabitants alive. They drove everyone—men, women, children and aged—into a barn and set it afire. The men nearest Hitler absorbed his same spirit. Himmler, for example, had a frenzied dedication to myths, folklore and the Utopian notion of a Teutonic race that would dominate the world. He pursued with viciousness the destruction of the Jewish race. Jews sought to hide in sewers and burned-out buildings. Sewers were opened up and smoke bombs were thrown into them. Those who sought to flee were caught and killed while others were exterminated in sewers.

Himmler's aim was not deportation but extermination of the Jewish people. Day after day, the trains departed for such places as Lublin-Maidanek, Auschwitz, Belsen and Dachau, stuffed with scarcely living bodies.

C.L. Sulzberger tells in his *American Heritage History of World War II* how the Allies arrived at these extermination centers and were stunned with shock and sorrow. Sulzberger adds,

> In these and other numerous concentration camps, Nazis incarcerated, starved and murdered more than 10 million human beings including at least 5,700,000 Jews.
>
> Often, most appalling of all, their corpses were boiled for soap. Their hair was used for mattresses and the fillings of their teeth for the system's gold hoard. Sometimes their tatooed

skins were used to decorate lamp shades.[226]

In describing Himmler, Felix Kersten, his physio-therapist, said,

There was a dichotomy in his nature. He carried out actions that were quite foreign to his nature. Though he had the mind of a schoolteacher, he was dominated by another Himmler. This other Himmler entered into realms which transcended the merely human and entered into another world.

Is It a Sin to Kill a Tyrant?

On July 20, 1944, Baron Ludwig von Leonrod asked Chaplain Hermann Wehrle, "Is it a sin to kill a tyrant?" The plot to assassinate Hitler had been developed by many top men such as Count Werner Von Der Schulenburg, who served as German ambassador to Moscow until 1941, Field Marshal Von Witzleben, who would have become Commander-in-Chief of the German Army if the assassination plot had been successful. The former mayor of Leipzig, Carl Goerdeler, was also among the men who planned Hitler's death, and we might also mention, Count von Stauffenberg, Chief of Staff to the Commander of the reserve army.

It was Stauffenberg who carried the two-pound bomb in his briefcase to Hitler's conference hut at Rastenburg. He set the briefcase under the large conference table at the feet of Adolph Hitler.

Excusing himself from the conference, he stepped outside at 12:41 P.M., and heard the deafening roar and witnessed the smoke and flames pour from the interior.

Hitler staggered from the building, his hair afire, his right arm partially paralyzed, his right leg burned, his eardrums damaged, leaving behind four dead or dying and two severely wounded men.

Retaliation

In retaliation for this attempt on his life, Sulzberger tells how Hitler had 15,000 arrested and 5,000 put to death. "Some of the more distinguished plotters were tried in specially constituted 'people's courts,'" he said. "These were humiliated and slowly strangled on meathooks."[227]

Man or Devil?

On the open page of William Peter Blatty's book, *The Exorcist,* are the names of Hitler's extermination centers. Apparently, the author offered these as evidence of satanic power.

Blatty, according to the press, would receive $15 million in royalties for his contribution to the film and book, *The Exorcist.*[228]

While his book, a mixture of filth, fiction and a few facts, was read by millions in the Western World, a single word such as "Dachau" offered more evidence of satanic power than the plot which involves a twelve-year-old child.

The Omen

Following the phenomenal reception of the film, *The Exorcist*, predicted to gross over $121 million, was a tidal wave of devil films.

Alan Ladd, Jr., (Divisional Head for Fox Films) said, "Almost every movie company has five or six devil films in the works."

Ned Tanen (MCA's Executive Vice President) stated, "Devil movies are the current staple. They even eclipsed the Western movies all over the world." MCA is preparing three demonic films. American International Pictures, Inc. has two devil films released and two more in production. Twentieth Century-Fox Films Corp. plans three sequels to *The Omen*.

The Omen cost $2.8 million to produce. The film has grossed thus far in box office returns $46.3 million. It is expected to gross over $100 million worldwide. Harvey Bernhard (producer of *The Omen*) attributes the success of the film to his theory that a growing number of people believe in evil forces like the devil and also to disasters like famine, floods and wars, which he says may lend some credence to the movie's thesis that the anti-Christ is at hand.

The Omen dealt with Satan and his power displayed on a wider scale. It referred to the Common Market of Brussels as the possible forerunner of the formation of the Holy Roman Empire, and a child of the devil, who would arise out of the world of politics, receiving orders directly from Satan, would establish a counterfeit kingdom on earth.[229]

11

The Devil's Number

Let him who has understanding reckon the number of the beast, for it is a human number, its number is six hundred and sixty-six (Rev. 13:18 RSV).

On the opening page of David Seltzer's sensational book, *The Omen*, he quotes the above passage from the Bible. While he does let his own imagination run wild in his book, which is also released in the film bearing the same title, he quotes freely from the book of Revelation.

Some of the fearful events suggested are too extreme to transpire, but others, such as the preparation for a worldwide number system, are most evident in today's strange society.

No One Today Winks

Prior to World War II, when as a young man speaking on the coming new world money system, I said,

I may live to see the day when men will not use

cash and currencies as at the present, but will buy or sell with a number system.

To some in the audience, my statement seemed too extreme to transpire, and the attorney in front of me turned and winked at the postmaster seated directly across the aisle. Today no one winks.

The Milestones Were Passed Rapidly

Shortly after the outbreak of the war, rationing was instituted by both the Allies and the Axis powers. In Germany if a farmer possessed an unregistered pig, he would be shot by the Nazis. England endured rationing for a total of thirteen years. In the most stringent period, a man received one egg a week and two ounces of beef. In America, the majority accepted rationing without complaint. While 60 million civilians and servicemen were dying, the rich and poor received equal allotments of many commodities under a system where the ration coupon took power over money as legal tender or a medium of exchange. The world indeed became number conscious when rationing was enforced.

While the war was still in progress, other major developments began to suggest a new direction for the entire world of finance. Man continued to pass milestone after milestone with such developments as:

The birth of the International Monetary Fund in 1944

The formation of the United Nations in 1945

The introduction of computers in 1945
Paper gold created in 1968
European Currency created by the Common
   Market in 1978.

Will the World Come Under Satanic Rule?

As men watched the world seemingly propelled toward a "one-world system" of government where humanity would homogenize into nothing more than numbers in a data bank linked internationally with satellites and computers, they were filled with fear.

Some read the writings of the famous Russian author Dostoyevsky who depicted in his novel, *Brothers Karamazov*, a world in the hands of a satanic ruler called a "beast."

Others who read more contemporary writings such as Seltzer's book, *The Omen*, asked, "Do the prophecies of the Bible actually state these things? If so, what does the Bible actually say?

The Words of the Prophets

There will be a world ruler with power over all nations.

Power was given him over all kindreds, and tongues, and nations. (Rev. 13:7)

The ruler is called a "Beast."

I . . . saw a beast rise up out of the sea. (Rev. 13:1)

Man that is in honor, and understandeth not, is like the beasts that perish. (Ps. 49:20)

As natural brute beasts . . . [they] speak evil of the things that they understand not. (2 Pet. 2:12)

The ruler arises out of the masses called the "sea."

I . . . saw a beast rise up out of the sea. (Rev. 13:1)

The wicked are like the troubled sea. (Isa. 57:20)

The waters . . . are peoples, and multitudes, and nations, and tongues. (Rev. 17:15)

The ruler will gain his power by deceit and flattery.

He shall enter peaceably. (Dan. 11:24)

He shall work deceitfully. (Dan. 11:23)

Shall he corrupt by flatteries. (Dan. 11:32)

The ruler will have power over the military.

Arms shall stand on his part. (Dan. 11:31)

Shall he honor the God of forces. (Dan. 11:38)

He shall act like a god.

> [He] shall do according to his will: and he shall
> exalt himself, and magnify himself above every
> god. (Dan. 11:36)

He shall make an image to himself and ask men to
worship it.

> And he hath power to give life unto the image of
> the beast, that the image of the beast should
> both speak, and cause that as many as would
> not worship the image of the beast should be
> killed. (Rev. 13:15)

The ruler will have power over the world's monetary
affairs.

> He shall have power over the treasures of gold
> and silver. (Dan. 11:43)

> He shall scatter . . . riches. (Dan. 11:24)

> Alas, alas . . . in one hour so great riches is
> come to naught. (Rev. 18: 16, 17)

> The merchants . . . shall weep . . . no man
> buyeth merchandise any more. (Rev. 18:11)

> Rich men, weep . . . riches are corrupted. . . .
> gold and silver is cankered. . . . Ye have heaped

treasure together for the last days. (James 5:1-3)

Under this ruler men buy and sell with a number.

> He causeth all, both small and great, rich and
> poor, free and bond, to receive a mark in their
> right hand, or in their foreheads:
> And that no man might buy or sell, save he that
> had the mark, or the name of the beast, or the
> number of his name. (Rev. 13:16-17)

The Beast of Brussels

While some read the prophecies of the Bible with intelligent understanding, others unfortunately only receive a strange conflation of fragmented quotations from the Bible mixed wild speculations of contemporary writers seeking to profit from books parading the sensational. Half-truths contained in such books as *The Omen,* produce only an atmosphere of fear and speculation. For many months there was a wave of publicity given to what was supposed to be a super-computer in Belgium. It was dubbed, "The Beast of Brussels."

When home in America, I was amazed to find a number of prominent news articles concerning "The Beast of Brussels." An example of such appeared in the *San Jose Mercury.* This article is entitled, "How About This?" It describes "the beast" as being a gigantic computer that occupies three floors of the administration building of the common market's headquarters. The article goes on to report that computer scientists are working on a master plan to assign numbers to each individual on earth. This number could be used for trading purposes—buying and selling.

The reporters suggest that a "digital number" could be "laser-tatooed" on the forehead or back of the hand. This "international mark" could do away with all currency. "No member could buy or sell without having an assignment of a digital mark," the article states.[230]

Cause for Concern

While living in Brussels, we watched men dig the foundations for the Common Market. We also witnessed the enthusiasm with which they talked of the "new system." I listened personally to the question asked of their leaders, "Do you plan to cancel the old currencies of Europe?"

There was no delay in the response. The answer was an unequivocal, "Yes."

While some smiled sympathetically at those who seemed prone to be overanxious over reports that at times were erroneous or exaggerated, the solemn truth was that the technology of the day was in truth moving ahead so fast, that what seemed wild fantasy in my youth, and even exaggerated stories at the present, were mild in comparison to what was really being developed.

On February 20, 1978, *Time* carried an article in which Dr. Robert Jastrow, director of NASA's Goddard Institute for Space Studies viewed a new relationship between computers and people. The caption on the article read,

TOWARD AN INTELLIGENCE BEYOND MAN'S.[231]

In speaking of the early computers, the article stated that these had limited capabilities such as a good memory. Computers of today, however, can "learn by experience, follow an argument, ask pertinent questions and write pleasing poetry and music."[232]

When reading Robert Jastrow's account of a computer that could speak in a manner that fooled men into thinking they were talking with a person, I paused to read in the Bible what John had written almost two thousand years earlier about a day when a world leader would have an image made of himself, an image which would speak. In Revelation 13, John wrote,

[He] deceiveth them that dwell on the earth . . . saying to them that dwell on the earth, that they should make an image to the beast. . . . And he hath power to give life unto the image of the beast, that the image of the beast should both speak. (Rev. 13:14, 15)

The Miraculous Growth of the Computer
The sudden explosion of computer technology in the present Space Age world is almost beyond comprehension.

In 1946

A computer was born that weighed 60,000 pounds and required 1,500 square feet of floor space to operate it.

In 1956

The computer had shrunk to 2,000 pounds in weight and required only 600 square feet of space.

In 1966

A computer more efficient than its predecessors had been reduced to the size of two office desks.

In 1976

A further improved computer would be no larger than a normal suitcase.

Today

Back in 1945, the first ENIAC computer required 18,000 vacuum tubes. Today, the circuitry needed for comparable performance could be housed inside one of those 18,000 tubes of the old model. The tiny desk-top models today could be reduced to still smaller dimensions if man's fingertips could be reduced accordingly to operate it.

The Speed of Performance

When the first computers appeared men talked in terms of seconds, and .001 milliseconds. Then on to .000001 microseconds, and .000000001 nano seconds. Still speed continued to .000000000001 pico seconds.

Bankers Favored Computers

For a number of years, bankers had striven to keep pace with economic growth that followed

World War II. Day after day, the struggle to process the checks written by Americans became ever more discouraging. By 1971, Americans were writing over 62 million checks daily. This meant that the banking service had to handle over 22 billion checks annually. When the projected studies for the future indicated that by 1981 Americans would be writing over 100,000,000 checks daily, and bank employees would have to handle annually almost 50,000,000,000 checks representing over $30,000,000,000,000, bankers cried, "We are being buried under paper!"

A study of the banking problems revealed that over 80 percent of the accounts carried balances of less than $1,000, and over half of all the checks written were for less than $25.00[233]

EFT

As the computer continued to become an ever-important factor in solving the banking frustrations of the Space Age, there were times when humor was mixed with the serious. The transfer of funds electronically soon became known as EFT.

There were others who viewed the role of the computer as something far more than a convenience for bankers and a boon in general. They feared its power was being expanded as a tool in the hands of too many agencies.

Big Brother

With the introduction of the computer into the private affairs of Americans, data centers sprang up almost overnight. TRW credit data with a goal to have records on anyone who had ever used credit added 50,000 names a week. The July issue of *Liberty* magazine declared that TRW had records on 70 million Americans and other institutions like Blue Cross of America had records on over 84 million.

NASA, according to one reporter, awarded a contract to Honeywell for a computer handling a 4500-foot-roll of tape which would be capable of filing up to twelve pages of data on each American on that one roll. Back in 1973, Stanley Aranoff writing in the *Los Angeles Times* stated that a reporter once conducted an experiment to discover how much information was recorded about a randomly selected individual at a data center. The center possessed information in the form of birth records, marriage records, health records, public school information, financial data about loans, armed service discharge records, etc.[234]

In 1978, the Carter Administration halted development of a nationwide $850 million computer for monitoring taxpayers.

The plan for the Tax Administration Service computer called for a large data-processing system with 8,300 terminals through which 48,300 IRS employees would have immediate access to the detailed tax records of individuals and corporations. It would have been Washington's biggest brother.[235]

Your Number
When recipients of Social Security were given a

number years ago, it was with the assurance that this harmless number was to be a very private possession of the individual and treated with respect and confidence. By 1943, the Social Security Number had become far more than a mere account number for the Social Security Administration. By 1961, it was required by government agencies, private industry, hospitals, educational institutions and all other record keepers. The same is also true in the ordinary world of daily commodities. A Fudge-Nut Bar, for example, may be known as "012345-54321."

Laser Scan Identifies Supermarket Items

Today in the market, one will see on all items a group of sixty or more lines or bars which release instant information to the computer when passed under the laser scan at the checker's counter.

The Universal Product Code, known as the UPC, was developed by the Universal Grocery Product Code Council, Inc.

The lines or bars on the various packages act as ten digits. The first five identify the producer of the item; the last five identify the particular item of his product line.[236]

No matter how the various items are placed on the checker's counter, the scanning beam reads its information with the cans, books, plastic packages placed in any position. In cooperation with the computer, it registers the price of the item for that particular day and any other pertinent information. Some pilot programs are being developed with the belief that the cost of the groceries purchased by the shopper, will be transmitted immediately to the local bank where the customer has his account, and the cost of his purchase deducted from his account without any exchange of cash or checks between the buyer and the seller.

A Number on the Hand or Head

When in Oklahoma City in 1975, I was interested in an article written in the *Oklahoma City Times* by R. Keith Farrell, a Washington State University professor. He states that the laser destroys skin pigments quite rapidly. He also reported that the laser is used to stitch a brand or number on livestock.[237]

In Texas, I asked a rancher if he was marking his cattle in this fashion and he told me he was.

I was especially interested in this method, for I had read an article in *Senior Scholastic* concerning a number placed by laser beam on man's forehead or hand. According to the record, the number placed painlessly on the individual would be invisible to the naked eye but legible under the designated scan light. The number once placed on the person would be as permanent as his fingerprints.[238]

When addressing a group of professional men in the Metropole Hotel in Brussels, Belgium, I was aware of their enthusiasm toward the new system that was advocated by leaders in Europe. A hush fell over the audience when I suggested that a fisherman named John, who had been banished as an exile to a tiny island off the coast of Asia Minor, had written concerning these things almost two thousand years previously. Many of my listeners apparently had not read the writings of John in the book of Revelation and were deeply moved when I read that John said,

> I was in the Spirit on the Lord's day, and heard behind me a great voice [saying]. . . . "I will show thee things which must be hereafter." (Rev. 1:10; 4:1)

The prophet described a day when a world ruler would have power over the monetary affairs of the world,

> He causeth all . . . to receive a mark in their right hand, or in their foreheads . . . that no man might buy or sell, save he that had the mark. (Rev. 13:16-17)

When the meeting adjourned and I drove from the heart of Brussels to our home at Rhode Saint Genese, I listened on the car radio to a spokesman from Frankfurt: "And today there is talk about placing a lifetime number on man's hand or head." The speaker on the Armed Forces Network heard in many countries, was not making this statement in relationship to scriptural prophecy, nor was he saying it in sarcasm; to him, it was merely a news item pertaining to the future. To me, it meant much more.

For over a decade bankers and technicians of Europe had been feverishly working to establish a new number system that would replace the antiquated currencies that were plaguing the international-trade world with confusion. I had listened to merchants tell of the nightmare of trying to plan international transactions when the exchange rates between dollars, francs, lira, guilders, marks and pounds changed radically from day to day. Bankers like Keller of Stuttgart and Verheek of Brussels said with a sigh, "We are being buried under mountains of paper; we must establish a common system with computer efficiency."

While I studied the faces around the table in the Metropole Hotel in the shadow of the Brussels Common Market, I asked, "Gentlemen, in your desire for the common number system, have you ever felt apprehension for the future as to who may control it?" For a moment there was silence. Some may have seen the film, *The Omen*, or have read the book by the same name, in which the author, David Seltzer, portrayed a world under a satanic ruler. After opening his book with a quotation from the book of Revelation pertaining to the worldwide number system, Seltzer proceeded to add some of his own imaginary scenes in such paragraphs as,

Your son, Mr. Thorn! Your son of Satan! He will establish his counterfeit kingdom here on earth, receiving his orders directly from Satan. . . . It is by means of a human personality entirely in his possession that Satan will wage his last and formidable offense. . . . The book of Revelation predicted it all.[239]

If the book of Revelation speaks of a satanic ruler ruling the world for a brief time by his control of the military and monetary powers of the world, thank God this is not all that the book says.

From this point on I concluded my address by telling the audience that the emphasis of the message of Revelation was not that of mankind in the hands of a world dictator empowered by Satan, but rather the coming of the true Messiah to overthrow the evil system that had held sway for a brief period.

"The world," I said, "is neither too small nor too poor to care for its family. There will come a day of peace, and according to the prophets that day is not as far distant as some might presently think."

12

New Money or None

**But they shall sit every man under his vine and
under his fig tree; and none shall make them
afraid: for the mouth of the Lord of hosts hath
spoken it. (Micah 4:4)**

The darkest hour is always just before the dawn.
No one declares this more forcefully than Peter who
writes:

We have also a more sure word of prophecy;
whereunto ye do well that ye take heed, as unto
a light that shineth in a dark place, until the day
dawn. (2 Pet. 1:19)

Each day the storm clouds on the world horizon
seemed to be growing darker. On July 10, 1979, I
picked up a copy of the *Oklahoma Journal* and read
on the front page:

WHAT IF U.S. ATTEMPTED TO TAKE OVER OIL FIELDS?[240]

The copy read:

Above the great Saudi desert, giant C-5A and C-130 cargo planes appear, carrying thousands of American paratroopers. The carrier Constellation is steaming toward the Persian Gulf and, in an hour, American warplanes will be clearing the way for marines to land.

The Saudi army is no match for the 110,000-person U.S. special strike force. Within two days the oil fields have been secured and Americans, including 5,000 civilian workers from Texas and Oklahoma, survey the area they have taken over.

They realize they have a problem. A pumping station near a main oil field has been blown up. It will take at least three months and $100 million to repair. Pipes that carry 20 percent of the oil to the tanker loading area have been blown apart.

Engineers estimate it will take at least four months to repair this damage. In another field a fire has been set. It has been blazing for a week now and officials say it will take at least five months to extinguish. And there are further threats of sabotage.

The oil fields are very easy to damage. An explosion in any of the vital areas, such as a pumping station or fire at a well, could close the facility for months.

The sequence of events is envisioned by U.S.

national security officials and military planners should the United States, in an all-out oil embargo, try to take over the Mideast oil fields against the will of the nations who own them.

National security officials say the United States is taking steps to beef up its ability to intervene in the Mideast and Persian Gulf. But the goal is not to invade in case of an oil embargo. Rather, the objective is to be ready to repel any external forces that may threaten the oil fields when a Mideast nation asks for help. The program is aimed specifically at deterring the Soviet Union from interfering in the oil fields.

The oil supply is extremely important to the United States and vital to Western Europe and Japan. Imported oil accounts for 49 percent of U.S. oil use, but 96 percent in Europe and 100 percent in Japan.

A key question is, at what point a U.S. response to an attack on a country such as Saudi Arabia would provoke Soviet intervention and affect other parts of the world.

Secretary of State Cyrus Vance has warned the appearance of overt military intervention in the area could be counterproductive and would increase tensions between the United States and its allies in the area. Other officials, including the authors of the Library of Congress study, say the United States does not have the resources to back up a commitment to intervene in the Mideast.

"Our active strategic reserves are too few to fight even a modest war in the Mideast without accepting calculated risks," the study says. "Even the best forces would probably prove insufficient against the Soviets, whose abilities to project offensive power beyond their frontiers have improved impressively in recent years."[241]

"Thank God," I said aloud, "that the prophet Ezekiel gives a brighter picture of this hour than the authors of the Library of Congress study, who suggest that we are unfit to fight even a modest war in the Mideast."

When writing on this theme in my study in Brussels, I was visited by Father Paul LeBeau from the University at Louven.

"What are you writing?" asked the priest.

"I am writing an article entitled, 'When God stops Russia,' " I replied, and I read again the words of Ezekiel, who told of Russia's invasion of the Mideast and how God said, "I will turn thee back and leave but a sixth part of thee."

"It is God who makes the difference in the balance of power," the priest said with a smile.

According to the prophets there is no doubt about it; Russia will be first to move in an effort to grab the prize of the Mideast. And by the authority of the same prophets they will be completely decimated as a power.

This momentous event will be followed by a shocked world falling quickly into a pattern of a world government controlled by one who enters the scene with flattery and with great ovation from the people, but becomes a tool of Satan.

This is the turning point of history. This is the termination of the Luciferian reign and his influence on earth.

At this dark moment, God's clock on the mantle of the ages strikes the hour for man's final deliverance from the sorrows brought by rebelling angels and men. One day a Washington reporter asked me for an interview in order that he might offer something to his press.

"What shall we call the article?" he asked.

"Why not label it, 'A Conservative Evangelical in Favor of World Government'?"

"Excellent," he answered with enthusiasm.

"But, may I add," I continued emphatically, "that I am not in favor of a world under the United Nations, nor in the hands of the global aristocracy, nor communists, nor a beast nor anti-Christ. I am in favor of a world described by the prophets in over 1860 passages of the Bible where God's Son, the true Messiah, will rule in peace."

The reporter wrote the article exactly as I gave it, and a headline that spread across the top of the page carried a picture and comments that spoke of God's promise of peace.

The Apostle Paul said, "He must reign, till he hath

put all enemies under his feet" (1 Cor. 15:25).

Clement, a father of the early church, wrote: "Wherefore let us expect the kingdom of God."

Luther said, "Let us expect our Redeemer's coming."

Calvin wrote, "The Scripture also enjoins us to look for the Advent of Christ."

John Knox said, "The Lord Jesus shall return."

John Wesley wrote 7,000 hymns, 5,000 of these carry the theme of Christ's return.

The Archbishop in England at the time of the coronation of the queen said, "I give thee this crown, O gracious lady, until He who deserves to wear it shall return."

Out of Zion Shall Go Forth the Law

And it shall come to pass in the last days. . . . he will teach us his ways, and we will walk in his paths: for out of Zion shall go forth the law, and the word of the Lord from Jerusalem. (Isa. 2:2, 3)

I think of the hundreds of Scriptures in which the prophets predicted a coming reign of peace and order when the law would go forth from Jerusalem. In considering these truths I naturally asked, "What did the prophets have to say concerning other cities of their day? Did they prophesy concerning others?" Indeed they did. With amazing detail they predicted the fall and disappearance of some of the most powerful cities of their time. In asking how reliable their prophecies had proven to be, I considered several of these cities of which they had spoken. First, I looked at Nineveh.

The Fall of Nineveh

Six hundred years before the birth of Christ, Nineveh was a city of tremendous power and grandeur. The walls of the city stood over 100 feet high, and fifty feet thick. On her walls were towers rising 200 feet above the ground, and in her walls were fifteen massive gates. Surrounding the city was a moat 150 feet wide. Such power! Such splendor! And yet the humble prophet Nahum had the audacity to say by the guidance of God's Spirit,

He will make an utter end [of Nineveh].
(Nahum 1:8)

Tyre Will Be Built No More

Ezekiel prophesied concerning the destruction of Tyre when the city was the mistress of the sea. For centuries Tyre had been the trade and commercial center of the world. But in 588 B.C. the prophet Ezekiel said concerning Tyre,

Therefore thus saith the Lord God; Behold I am against thee, O Tyrus, . . . and they shall destroy the walls of Tyrus and break down her towers: I will also scrape her dust from her, and make her like the top of a rock. It shall be a

place for the spreading of nets. . . . Thou shalt
be no more: though thou be sought for, yet shalt
thou never be found again. (Ezek. 26:1-21)

When Alexander the Great came, long after
Ezekiel had uttered these prophetic words, he broke
down the walls and towers, exactly as predicted, and
scraped the rubble into the sea. The rocks on which
the city had been built were left so completely bare,
the fishermen used the site as a place to spread their
nets. It remains this way still today.

I Will Make Samaria a Heap of Ruins
When we stood on the site of ancient Samaria we
recalled the words written by the prophet Micah in
725 B.C.,

I will make Samaria as an heap of the field . . .
I will pour down the stones thereof into the
valley, and will discover the foundations. (Mic.
1:6)

Samaria was the capital of the northern Hebrew
kingdom of Israel. It had been the city in which
Ahab had his ivory palace and was one of the great
cities of her day. Today a few pillars stand as a
reminder of her ancient beauty, but the stones in the
valley and the vineyards on the hill bear mute
testimony to the accuracy of the prophecy.

Babylon Will Never Be Inhabited

Of all the cities that should have remained, Babylon should still be in existence. The magnificent city covering 196 square miles was surrounded by walls 311 feet high, eighty-seven feet wide, and a moat of thirty feet.

Her 100 gates that shone like fires in the sunset, her riverbed of paved, dyed brick, her hanging gardens that towered 450 feet into the heavens made her a wonder of the world. And yet at the height of her strength Isaiah wrote (in 712 B.C.),

And Babylon, the glory of kingdoms, the beauty of the Chaldees' excellency, shall be as when God overthrew Sodom and Gomorrah.

It shall never be inhabited, neither shall it be dwelt in from generation to generation; neither shall the Arabian pitch tent there; neither shall the shepherds make their fold there. (Isa. 13:19-20)

Travelers report that Babylon is totally without habitation even by Bedouins. Some say that superstitions among Arabs prevent them from pitching their tents there, and the soil is such that it will not produce suitable pastures for the flocks of the shepherds.

Jerusalem Shall Be Built

While the prophets predicted the passing of such cities as Nineveh, Tyre, Samaria, Babylon, Gaza-Ashkelon, Sidon, Thebes, Memphis, Jericho and others, much was written concerning Jerusalem being rebuilt and becoming the final center of world government.

Some historians estimate that over a period of 3,000 years Jerusalem was under siege over thirty times. Even when destroyed by invaders, the prophets told how and when it would be rebuilt. A classic example of such prophecy comes from Isaiah, when in 712 B.C. he named king Cyrus 175 years before the king was born, and described in detail how he would order the rebuilding of the city and temple.

The prophet, speaking in the first person as a mouthpiece of God, said,

I have even called thee by thy name: I have surnamed thee, though thou hast not known me. (Isa. 45:4)

And describing his work he said:

He . . . shall perform all my pleasure: even saying to Jerusalem, Thou shalt be built; and to the temple, Thy foundation shall be laid. (Isa. 44:28)

750,000,000,000,000,000,000,000 to 1

Cyrus was by no means the only king who was described by the prophets. Between 2,000 B.C. and 400 B.C. the birth and deeds of at least forty other kings were mentioned. In his book, *Scientific*

222

Investigation of the Old Testament, Robert Dick
Wilson estimates the predictions made concerning
these kings could not easily have been fulfilled by
mere chance. If such were the case, the answer would
be that the odds were 750,000,000,000,000,000,000,000
to 1 that these prophecies could have been fulfilled
by chance.[242]

> **100,000,000,000,000,000,000,000,000,000,000,**
> **000,000,000,000,000,000,000,000,000,000,000,**
> **000,000,000,000,000,000,000,000,000,000,000,**
> **000,000,000,000,000,000,000,000,000,000,000,**
> **000,000,000,000,000,000,000,000,000—to—1**

When considering the prophecies of the Old
Testament concerning Christ, Peter Stoner, mathematician and astronomer, considered first of all eight
specific prophecies. He said,

> We find that the chance that any man might
> have lived down to the present time and fulfilled
> all eight prophecies would be 1 in 10^{17} or a
> billion times a billion to one.

But Stoner, the mathematician, did not stop at
eight prophecies; he went on to consider forty-eight
prophecies and said,

> We find that the chance that any man could
> have fulfilled all 48 prophecies to be one chance
> in 10^{157} or to say it in trillions, it would be:
> 100,000 times a trillion times a trillion times a

223

trillion times a trillion times a trillion times a
trillion times a trillion times a trillion times a
trillion times a trillion times a trillion times a
trillion times a trillion times a trillion times a
trillion times a trillion times a trillion—to—1.[243]

Peter Stoner need not have stopped at even forty-eight prophecies. He could have gone on to examine the 300 Old Testament prophecies that were fulfilled in the life of Christ.

Peter Stoner, who wrote *Science Speaks,* taught at the University of California and later served as chairman of the science division at Westmont College.

I noticed that Harold Hartzler wrote the introduction to Peter Stoner's book, *Science Speaks.* H. Harold Hartzler was one of America's most esteemed astronomers. Regarding Stoner's writing, Hartzler said,

The manuscript for *Science Speaks* has been carefully reviewed by a committee of the American Scientific Affiliation members and by the Executive Council of the same group and has been found in general to be dependable and accurate in regard to the scientific material presented.[244]

I Will Come Again
The prophets not only predicted the first Advent of Christ's coming; they also wrote much concerning

His Second Coming. Micah, who speaks of His birth in Bethlehem, declared:

> But thou, Bethlehem Ephratah . . . yet out of thee shall he come forth unto me that is to be ruler in Israel; whose goings forth have been from of old, from everlasting. (Mic. 5:2)

The prophets wrote concerning His first and His second coming. In describing His first appearing as Savior of the world, they wrote such Scriptures as: "They pierced my hands and my feet" (Ps. 22:16) and "They part my garments among them, and cast lots upon my vesture" (Ps. 22:18).

Christ realized that the prophets had predicted all of these details concerning His life and ministry. After His resurrection, when He walked with Cleophas and Cephas, He said,

> O fools, and slow of heart to believe all that the prophets have spoken:
> Ought not Christ to have suffered these things, and to enter into his glory?
> And beginning at Moses and all the prophets, he expounded unto them in all the scriptures the things concerning himself. (Luke 24:25-27)

But Christ not only explained how He came the first time to fulfill the prophecies pertaining to His work of redemption. He also declared in unmistakable terms that He would return. For example, He said, "The Son of man shall come in the glory of his Father" (Matt. 16:27), and "I will come again" (John 14:3).

Robert Morris Page, the physicist who invented pulsation radar, became so convinced of the miraculous utterances of the prophets concerning Christ and the manner in which they were fulfilled that he wrote,

> The authenticity of the writings of the prophets, though the men themselves are human, is established by such things as the prediction of highly significant events far in the future that could be accomplished only through a knowledge obtained from a realm which is not subject to the laws of time as we know them.
>
> One of the great evidences is the long series of prophecies concerning Jesus the Messiah. These prophecies extend hundreds of years prior to the birth of Christ. They include a vast amount of detail concerning Christ himself, His nature and the things He would do when He came—things which to the natural world, or the scientific world remain to this day completely inexplicable.[245]

For a number of years I had read the writings of Page. His credentials were impressive. B.S., Hamline University; M.S., George Washington University; D.Sc., Hamline University. He served with the

Naval Research Laboratory, Washington, D.C. He completed first pulse radar in the world for detection of aircraft. He received the U.S. Navy Distinguished Civilian Service Award, the Presidential Certificate of Merit, IRE Fellowship Harry Diamond Memorial Award, Stuart Ballantyne Medal of the Franklin Institute and is a holder of thirty-seven patents, mostly in radar.

I naturally found myself asking, "If men of the stature of Peter Stoner, Harold Hartzler and Robert Morris Page were convinced that the prophecies concerning Christ's first coming were so scientifically proven to be supernatural and valid, would it not be logical to believe that the prophecies pertaining to His return to rule in peace would be equally true?

When I shared these thoughts with a friend, he asked, "What does this have to do with a theme such as *New Money or None?*

"Everything," I replied. "Today the world is in a state of total confusion. The prophets predict the conditions we see. Governments are failing. Systems are crumbling. And many of the intellectual pundits of the world offer man no hope for his future. The Bible declares that the old systems of man will pass, and a number system will be introduced, but not for long. Christ will come and take over the reins of power, and will bring suddenly an era of peace. The prophet John says there will be a shout of triumph."

The kingdoms of this world are become the kingdoms of our Lord, and of his Christ; and he shall reign forever and ever. (Rev. 11:15)

227

When on earth, Christ wept because many could not understand He came first to take away the sin of the world, and that He would not at that time establish the throne of David.

On March 26, 1979, we were in Israel when the peace treaty was signed between Egypt and Israel. In a telecast produced in Jerusalem on the Mount of Olives, and relayed back to America by satellite, I said, "Two thousand years ago on this very spot Jesus looked over the city and said,

If thou hadst known even thou, at least in this thy day, the things which belong unto thy peace! but now they are hid from thine eyes. (Luke 19:42)

The crowd that waved the palm fronds and spread their garments in the way that day thought He had come then to fulfill the promise to establish the earthly kingdom. They cried,

Blessed be the King that cometh. (Luke 19:38)
Blessed be the kingdom of our father David. (Mark 11:10)

Christ knew it was not the time to establish such a kingdom. He said,

Jerusalem shall be trodden down of the Gentiles until the times of the Gentiles be fulfilled. (Luke 21:24)

The prophet Daniel depicted the final formation of man's kingdom that concluded the period known as "The Times of the Gentiles." He spoke of the world powers in our day that would be divided, partly strong and partly broken and not cleaving one to another. He also said:

In the days of these kings shall the God of heaven set up a kingdom which shall never be destroyed: and the kingdom shall not be left to other people . . . and it shall stand forever. (Dan. 2:44)

Daniel was careful to state that his predictions of the empires that would rise and fall, until the end of the age, were not given from the source of his own natural wisdom. He said,

This secret is not revealed to me for any wisdom that I have more than any living. . . . But there is a God in heaven that revealeth secrets, and maketh known . . . what shall be in the latter days. (Dan. 2:30, 28)

Prime Minister Benjamin Disraeli

Prime Minister Benjamin Disraeli, intimate friend of the famous family of Rothschilds said,

The time will come when countless myriads will find music in the songs of Zion and solace in the parables of Galilee. . . . The pupil of Moses may ask himself whether all the princes of the House of David have done so much for the Jews as the Prince who was crucified?[246]

Regarding Disraeli, David Ben-Gurion, Prime Minister of Israel, said,

Benjamin Disraeli, one of the greatest nineteenth-century statesmen was a Jew, who though baptized as a child, always remained proud of his Jewish heritage.[247]

Tolstoy, called by Alexander Solzhenitsyn "The King of Russian literature," wrote concerning the Jew:

The Jew is that sacred being who has brought down from Heaven the Everlasting Fire, and has enlightened with it the entire world. He is the religious source, spring, and fountain out of which all the rest of the peoples have drawn their beliefs and their religions.

The Jew is a pioneer of liberty. Even in olden days, when the people were divided into two distinct classes—slaves and masters, even so long ago, the Law of Moses prohibited the keeping in bondage for more than six years any person who willingly came to accept the Jewish practice. . . .

The Jew is an emblem of civil and religious tolerance. "Love the stranger and the sojourner," Moses commanded. "Because you have been strangers in the land of Egypt."

While Disraeli contended that Jews and Christians had the Old Testament in common, he added, "Christians believe the Old Testament the same as the Jews but they believe the New Testament also."

Regarding Paul's writings in the New Testament, Ben-Gurion, although not accepting Paul's position, writes:

Christianity grew out of Judaism. Jesus probably differed little from other Jews of his generation.

In the beginning Saul (later called Paul) was a fanatic opponent of the Christian sect that developed in Jerusalem but after he "saw the light" on the Damascus road, he gave Christianity a new direction. . . . From a Messianic vision that prophesied redemption for both the Jewish nation and the world, he based Christianity on a faith in a divine redemption brought by a Messiah who supposedly had already come.[248]

No one loved the Jewish people more than Paul who spoke of himself as a "Hebrew of the Hebrews" (Phil. 3:5) and said concerning his people,

Who are Israelites; to whom pertaineth the adoption, and the glory, and the covenants, and the giving of the law, and the service of God, and the promises. (Rom. 9:4)

Paul read the words of Isaiah the prophet:

It is a light thing that thou shouldest be my servant to raise up the tribes of Jacob, and to restore the preserved of Israel: I will also give thee for a light to the Gentiles, that thou mayest be my salvation unto the end of earth. (Isa. 49:6)

Paul was persuaded that in His first coming, Christ came to unite all into one family of faith. He told the Ephesians in his letter,

How that by revelation he made known unto

me . . . that the Gentiles should be fellow-heirs
and of the same body. (Eph. 3:3, 6)

John, too, speaks of a New Jerusalem where on the
gates are written, "The names of the twelve tribes of
the children of Israel" (Rev. 21:12).
And on the foundations are written, "The names
of the twelve apostles" (Rev. 21:14).
And in further description of this New Jerusalem,
John says,

And the kings of the earth do bring their glory
and honor into it. . . . And they shall bring the
glory and honor of the nations into it. (Rev.
21:24, 26)

The Glory and Honor of the Nations

When the prophet Isaiah described Christ in His
first appearing as Savior of mankind he said,

He is despised and rejected of men; a man of
sorrows, and acquainted with grief: we hid as it
were our faces from him; he was despised, and
we esteemed him not. (Isa. 53:3)

But this is not the picture of Christ that is
portrayed by the prophets on His return. In the
opening chapter of Revelation, John heard a voice
saying, "I am Alpha and Omega, the first and the
last" and when John turned at the sound of this voice
he saw Christ whose glory overwhelmed him. He
writes:

I saw . . . one like unto the Son of man. . . .
His head and his hairs were white like wool . . .

and his eyes were as a flame of fire. (Rev. 1:13-14)

John was so overwhelmed at what he saw that he said, "When I saw him, I fell at his feet as dead" (Rev. 1:17).

The prophet Daniel, like John, had a similar experience. Daniel writes:

I beheld till the thrones were cast down, and the Ancient of days did sit, whose garment was white as snow, and the hair of his head like the pure wool. . . . And there was given him dominion, and glory, and a kingdom, that all people, nations, and languages, should serve him: his dominion is an everlasting dominion, which shall not pass away. (Dan. 7:9, 14)

There can be no mistake about the clarity of the message of the prophets. John writes: "The kingdoms of this world are become the kingdoms of our Lord and of his Christ; and he shall reign for ever and ever" (Rev. 11:15).

His kingdom will be one of power and justice. John says, "In righteousness he doth judge. . . . (Rev. 19:11) . . . and he shall rule them with a rod of iron" (Rev. 19:15).

Under His rule John says, there will be, "The healing of the nations" (Rev. 22:2).

All Things New

In the climactic portion of John's vision of the future he hears the blessed announcement:

He that sat upon the throne said, Behold, I make all things new. (Rev. 21:5)

Under His rule wars will cease, and men no longer will labor for that "which is not meat." No longer will men spend one billion dollars daily on arms and armies. It would be difficult to imagine under His rule of justice a Caesar's Palace in Las Vegas paying Ann-Margaret $200,000 a week, Sammy Davis $225,000 weekly, and Frank Sinatra a million dollars annually to appear for only four weeks of that year in Caesar's Palace.[249]

Christ did not suggest that every man would receive an equal allotment, but He did say it would be a just allotment, based on the individual's faithfulness or merit. He spoke of one servant receiving ten talents, another five and still another, one.

The Apostle Paul declared:

Every man shall receive his own reward according to his own labor. (1 Cor. 3:8)

If He reigns in righteousness, it would hardly seem right that half of the world's laborers receive only two dollars weekly and a quarter of earth's wage earners make only fifty dollars a year.

When He reigns with a rod of iron and heals the nations it will not be likely that a population numbering half the population of the city of Chicago will be allowed to control the flow of oil in their country in a manner that exploits especially the oil-poor nations of earth.

Intelligent men like R. Buckminster Fuller have said that the proper control and distribution of earth's resources could supply every man on earth with abundance. One ambitious mathematician sought to compute the total value of earth's resources, and after assessing his estimate of the value of the gold, minerals, oil, timber, fruit and grain, etc. he declared the combined worth to be one decillion dollars. For my own interest I wrote down this figure of $1,000,000,000,000,000,000,000,000,000, 000,000 and divided the same by the population of the world which is over 4,000,000,000, and realized this would give every person on earth a claim to riches worth $250,000,000,000,000,000,000,000. If the mathematician's estimate was 250 billion times wrong, there should at least be grounds to say that the earth possesses adequate wealth to care for all if properly handled.

Within recent years, science has made tremendous steps forward even as Daniel the prophet said, at the time of the end, "Knowledge shall be increased" (Dan. 12:4).

When delivering an address to a research department of the government I said, "Gentlemen, God the Creator never made this world with rivers that flow, birds that sing, flowers that blossom and fruit that ripens as a home for man just to have it blown up by fanatics. He never willed that man write a final chapter in the fumes of pollution nor die in a bone yard of famine. The prophets declare that He will destroy those who destroy the earth and He will make "all things new."

The Creator

When Borman, Lovell and Anders made their voyage into space in Apollo 8, there was a long period of silence when men on earth waited anxiously for word from the heavens. Then, on that Christmas Eve of 1968, their voices were heard clearly from a distance of 237,000 miles from earth. And the first words spoken by these brave men in the heavens were: "In the beginning God created the heavens and the earth."

They were not ashamed to read the story of creation from the Bible. Nor were many of the other astronauts, like Eugene Cernan who looked back at earth and saw it "as God the Creator beheld it in the hour of creation." One of the most encouraging sights in this hour of confusion and danger, is man's willingness to look to his Maker for divine aid. When naming the sorrows that would close this age, Christ not only defined the troublesome times, He also said,

> When these things begin to come to pass, then look up, and lift up your heads; for your

redemption draweth nigh. (Luke 21:28)

God and Science

On February 5, 1979, an impressive article appeared in *Time* magazine, entitled, "In the Beginning: God and Science."[250]

It read:

Sometime after the enlightenment, science and religion came to a gentleman's agreement. Science was for the real world: machines, manufactured things, medicines, guns, moon rockets. Religion was for everything else, the immeasurable: morals, sacraments, poetry, insanity, death and some residual forms of politics and statesmanship. Religion became in both senses immaterial. . . . This hostile distinction between religion and science has softened in the last third of the twentieth century, . . . perhaps the most extraordinary sign of that intimacy is what appears to be an agreement between religion and science about certain facts concerning creation of the universe.

According to the *Book of Genesis,* the universe began in a single, flashing act of creation—the divine intellect willed all into being, *ex nihilo.* Most astronomers now accept that the universe had an instant creation. . . . sounds very much like the story that the Old Testament has been telling all along.[251]

Faith in the Creator

Long ago the ancient philosopher Job wrote:

But ask now the beasts, and they shall teach thee; and the fowls of the air, and they shall tell thee:

Or speak to the earth and it shall teach thee: and the fishes of the sea shall declare unto thee.

Who knoweth not in all these that the hand of the Lord hath wrought this? (Job 12:7-9)

How many times have men marveled at the millions of miracles in this created world? The world is the right size, turning at the right speed to control the gases of our atmosphere that are fit for man to breathe. It has the proper balance of 71 percent ocean and 29 percent land to sustain life, and the oceans themselves are a mystery. When 200 oceanographers compiled a volume of their research, they closed the last page by saying, "The oceans are His and He made them."

The earth is the right distance from the sun and turns on its axis at the proper speed to retain the right temperature to sustain life. The moon is the right size and distance from earth to control the tides of the oceans which also play an important role in sustaining life. And the meteorites invading our atmosphere daily are also the right number to burn into star dust.

And if man looks at the fish and fowls, as Job suggested, they too illustrate a wisdom controlling them, a wisdom that is higher than the human.

In Europe, the little German warbler, weighing less than one ounce, will migrate to Africa all alone After flying thousands of miles on a course it has never traveled before, it will go to the nest its mother built in Africa the year before.

And from the Rhine River, the eel may swim thousands of miles to an area of the Atlantic off the coast of Norfolk, Virginia; there it will deposit its young and return. Many months later the tiny eel that had been growing and swimming on its journey back to Europe, will return to the very waters the mother occupied.

At the conclusion of an address I delivered to men of science in government I reminded them of the comment by Albert Einstein who said God did not "throw dice." In other words, these mysteries did not occur by mere "chance."

If man can see design in his natural world, then logic demands a designer. When the great Creator at the close of the age destroys those who destroy the earth, He will do it suddenly (1 Thess. 5:3).

The Lord Whom Ye Seek Shall Suddenly Come

Today men talk about coming destruction, and suggest that the cities of a nation could be leveled in seventeen minutes. The prophets of the Bible also speak of the sudden destruction that will come, but unlike modern prophets of the world who term this "the end," the prophets of God declare that this marks only the end of Lucifer's influence on earth,

239

the end of rebelling man's regime, and the beginning of a world of peace under a ruling Christ. And just as the prophets speak of sudden destruction they also speak of sudden redemption of man and his world. Malachi writes:

The Lord, whom ye seek, shall suddenly come to his temple . . . who may abide the day of his coming? (Mal. 3:1-2)

The prophet Isaiah not only speaks of the "day of vengeance of our God" (Isa. 61:2). He also says:

I will greatly rejoice in the Lord . . . God will cause righteousness and praise to spring forth before all the nations. (Isa. 61:10-11)

And he adds,

They shall build the old wastes, they shall raise up the former desolations, and they shall repair the waste cities, the desolations of many generations. (Isa. 61:4)

God or Man?

In His first public discourse delivered in His home town of Nazareth, Christ quoted from the words of Isaiah. Luke writes:

And he came to Nazareth, where he had been brought up: and, as his custom was, he went into the synagogue on the sabbath day, and stood up for to read.

And there was delivered unto him the book of the prophet Isaiah.

And when he had opened the book, he found the place where it was written,

The Spirit of the Lord is upon me, because he hath anointed me to preach the gospel to the poor; he hath sent me to heal the broken-hearted, to preach deliverance to the captives, and recovering of sight to the blind, to set at liberty them that are bruised,

To preach the acceptable year of the Lord.

And he began to say unto them, This day is this scripture fulfilled in your ears.

And all they in the synagogue, when they heard these things, were filled with wrath,

And rose up and thrust him out of the city, and led him unto the brow of the hill whereon their city was built, that they might cast him down headlong. (Luke 4:16-19, 21, 28, 29)

The audience at Nazareth reacted as they did to His statement because they knew He claimed to be the fulfillment of Isaiah's promise of the Messiah. When Christ asked His own followers:

Whom say ye that I am? (Matt. 16:15)

Peter replied:

Thou art the Christ, the Son of the living God. (Matt. 16:16)

And Jesus answered and said unto him:

Blessed art thou Simon Barjona: for flesh and blood hath not revealed it unto thee, but my Father which is in heaven. (Matt. 16:17)

Men who failed to recognize Him as the Son of God sought to stone Him because He made himself equal with God. He said:

I and my Father are one. Then the Jews took up stones again to stone Him. Jesus answered them, Many good works have I showed you from my Father; for which of those works do ye stone me? The Jews answered him saying . . . because that thou, being a man, makest thyself God. (John 10:30-33)

It is little wonder that those in His day said never man spake like this man. He said:

Verily, verily, I say unto you, Before Abraham was, I am. (John 8:58)
He that hath seen me hath seen the Father. (John 14:9)

When asked at His trial:

"Art thou the Christ, the Son of the Blessed?" (Mark 14:61)

He answered:

"I am: and ye shall see the Son of man sitting on the right hand of power." (Mark 14:62)

Those who have studied His life and His claims must declare it is impossible to be neutral concerning Jesus Christ. He was either a liar, a lunatic or all that He declared himself to be.

C.S. Lewis Concerning Christ

C.S. Lewis, who was a Cambridge professor and once an agnostic, said:

I am trying here to prevent anyone from saying the really foolish thing that people often say about Him: "I am ready to accept Jesus as a great moral teacher, but I don't accept His claims to be God." That is one thing we must not say. A man who was merely a man and said the sort of things that Jesus said would not be a great moral teacher. He would either be a lunatic—on a level with the man who says he is a poached egg—or else he would be the devil of hell. You must make your choice. Either this man was, and is, the Son of God: or else a madman or something worse.[252]

Testimony of Simon Greenleaf

Simon Greenleaf was the famous Royall Professor of Law at Harvard University who succeeded Justice Joseph Story as the Dane Professor of Law upon Story's death.

H.W.H. Knott says of this great authority in jurisprudence:

To the efforts of Story and Greenleaf is to be ascribed the rise of the Harvard Law School to its eminent position among the legal schools of the United States.[253]

Greenleaf produced a famous work entitled: *A Treatise On the Law of Evidence.* This is still considered to be the greatest single authority on evidence in the entire literature of legal procedure.

Chief Justice Fuller of the United States Supreme Court once asserted (about Greenleaf):

He is the highest authority in our courts.[254]

Greenleaf wrote:

If a close examination of the evidences of Christianity may be expected of one class of men more than another, it would seem incumbent upon lawyers who make the law of evidence one of our peculiar studies. Our profession leads us to explore the mazes of falsehood, to detect its artifices, to pierce its thickest veils, to follow and expose its sophistries, to compare the statements of different witnesses with severity, to discover truth and separate it from error.[255]

Regarding Christ and His teaching, Greenleaf wrote:

The religion of Jesus Christ . . . not only solicits the grave attention of all, to whom its doctrines are presented, but it demands their cordial belief as a matter of vital concernment. These are no ordinary claims; and it seems hardly possible for a rational being to regard them with even a subdued interest; much less to treat them with mere indifference and contempt. If not true, they are little else than the pretensions of a bold impostor. . . . but if they are well founded and just they can be no less than the high requirements of heaven, addressed by the voice of God to the reason and understanding of man . . . such was the estimate taken of religion, even the religion of pagan Rome, by one of the greatest lawyers of antiquity, when he argued that it was either nothing at all or everything. *Aut undique religionem tolle, aut usquequa que conserva.*[256]

In referring to the apostles who wrote the Gospels, Greenleaf said,

They had every possible motive to review carefully the grounds of their faith, and the evidences of the great facts and truths which they asserted. . . . And their writings show them to have been men of vigorous understandings. If then, their testimony was not true, there was no possible motive for this fabrication.[257]

William Lecky, The Great Historian
William Lecky, the great historian, said concerning Christ:

245

Amid all the sins and failings, amid all the priestcraft and persecution and fanaticism that have defaced the church, it has preserved in the character and example of its founder (Jesus), an enduring principle of regeneration.[258]

Encyclopedia Britannica

Encyclopedia Britannica devotes over 20,000 words to the person of Jesus which is more than is given to Aristotle, Alexander the Great, Cicero, Julius Caesar, or Napoleon.[259]

Napoleon Bonaparte

Napoleon said:

The nature of Christ's existence is mysterious, I admit; but this mystery meets the wants of man—reject it and the world is an inexplicable riddle; believe it, and the history of our race is satisfactorily explained.[260]

Again Napoleon said:

I know men; and I tell you that Jesus Christ is not a man. Superficial minds see a resemblance between Christ and the founders of empires, and the gods of other religions. That resemblance does not exist. There is between Christianity and whatever other religions, the distance of infinity. . . . His religion is a revelation from an intelligence which certainly is not that of man.[261]

Rousseau

Rousseau asks:

Can the person whose history the Gospels relate be himself a man?

He answers:

If the life and death of Socrates are those of a philosopher, the life and death of Jesus Christ are those of a God.[262]

The Testimony of My Father

On some maps of Ireland one may find the name Cantelon (or the older spelling of the name Cantillon) written in red across the southwest corner. When the Anglo-Norman family settled in County Kerry long ago they built the original castle at Ballyheigue. For over 400 years, nine generations of Cantelons lived in Kerry and later had estates at Ballyorgan near Limerick. In the early 1840s four Cantelon brothers came to Canada and settled near Toronto. The lure of the West, however, was too much for my father's father who moved on to Manitoba. Winnipeg, called the gateway to the West, was little more than an oversized trading center in those years. The streets were unpaved, and reflected all of the characteristics of a pioneer settlement.

It was west of Winnipeg, on the banks of the Souris River, where my father grew from boyhood to young manhood. He was oldest of five sons and three daughters who all grew up in this paradise of virgin land. The forests abounded with game, the ravines with wild fruit. The neighbors were eager to join in cricket matches in the springtime or dance the winter nights away.

One thing, however was lacking in this French-Irish family, they had no thought or time for God; life seemed complete without Him.

The spiritual change that took place in my father's life occurred one winter night in Winnipeg. Entering his hotel room he noticed that something had been added in his absence; a Bible had been left on his table. It was about this time that a group of men, choosing the name "The Gideons" organized to place Bibles in hotels; presumably this was one of the very first to be placed in such a manner.

Carelessly, my father opened it. It was a strange book to him. Formal religion had held little attraction for his family and the Bible, like church attendance, had not been a part of their life.

When he began to read words written by the prophet Isaiah, his interest continued to increase and so did his inward struggle. If there was a God who was more than the God of nature who gave his Son for man's redemption, how could he know Him, how could he be sure?

He looked at the light switch on the wall and said, "I don't understand all the natural mysteries of life. No man can fully explain how in the wind and water power can be harnessed to light a room but I can press a button and change darkness to light." With the same simple faith he prayed, "Dear God, I confess I know little about you, but you tell me that I could approach you personally through the name of your Son, Christ. I ask you to forgive my sin and grant me your Spirit."

A few days later he called a reunion of his brothers, sisters and parents. When he shared with them the newfound experience, he did not have to say a great deal; all could see he was different. Together, the entire family knelt to pray and arose transformed, in what Christ called "the new birth."

Today in America, magazines as widely read as *Time* fill pages with testimonies of lives transformed through the born-again experience. In bold letters on the cover of the Oct. 25, 1976 edition of *Time,* we read the words: "BORN AGAIN."[263]

My Father and Depression

Between the years of his conversion and the collapse of the market that ushered in the Great Depression, my father prospered. The home and family, however, did not occupy his first priority or care; God's work came first. Many times he read the words of Christ recorded by St. Matthew:

Behold the fowls of the air: for they sow not, neither do they reap, nor gather into barns; yet your heavenly Father feedeth them. Are ye not much better than they? Consider the lilies of the field, how they grow; they toil not, neither do they spin: And yet I say unto you, That even Solomon in all his glory was not arrayed like one of these. Wherefore, if God so clothe the

grass of the field, which today is, and tomorrow
is cast into the oven, shall he not much more
clothe you, O ye of little faith?
But seek ye first the kingdom of God and his
righteousness; and all these things shall be
added unto you. (Matt. 6:26, 28-30, 33)

Taking the words of Christ literally, my father
began to strive to seek first the kingdom of God and
His righteousness. His giving to the church and the
work of Christ became the foremost concern of his
life. It was not merely giving his tithe, as suggested in
the Scriptures; it was much more. And "Money," he
would say, "is not the only factor of importance; a
man's time is also important, and the Sabbath is not
to be considered a holiday but a holy day."

As a lad I was raised in such an atmosphere, but
there was no feeling ever of disdain or rebellion for
my father's faith and way of life. He loved his family
greatly, but it was obvious he loved God more.
There were those who considered him an extremist
for giving so liberally to God's work, but as the
depression deepened, this criticism changed to
wonder and curiosity.

As a youth, I once overheard some older people
talking about my father. One said, "E.J. Cantelon
must surely have a secret source. He continues to
give even in these dark days of depression while
many are forced to take government aid and barely
exist." A teen-age friend was standing by me, who
also heard this comment. He asked, "Is it true that
your father has some secret source of revenue?"

"It seems to be so," I replied slowly. "It really is no secret; it is merely my father's simple faith that Christ meant what He said when He declared, 'If we seek first the kingdom of God and His righteousness all other things will be added.' "

More Precious Than Gold That Perisheth

The Apostle Peter speaks of our faith that is "More precious than of gold that perisheth" (1 Pet. 1:7).

When the Great Depression began in 1929 many astute people, fearing that the American dollar would lose its value or gold backing, began to buy gold. Through the centuries men had always chosen gold as the most preferred possession. It was considered man's most secure treasure. But how helpless they were to retain their gold. When Franklin Roosevelt demanded, under the threat of fines and imprisonment, that men turn their gold to the government, they had to comply with his order.

In the postwar days in Germany when food was scarce, an industrialist from East Germany arrived in Frankfurt hungry and destitute. He told me how he offered his gold ring for a quarter pound of margarine. His offer was treated with scorn by the one who said, "Keep your ring, I can eat my margarine." There have been times in the past, when gold has not been as secure as some thought.

Through the years of depression there seemed almost countless times when the needs of our family were met not with hoarded gold, but in ways that seemed miraculous. The needs which varied were supplied in manners that even money could not have bought. Many others in those dark days spoke with despair and satire.

I Traded My Farm for This Cow

I recalled hearing a farmer on the street of the village telling his friends that on his way to town he met a man leading a cow.

"Where did you get your cow?" he asked.

"I traded my farm for it," was the reply. "And I played a mean trick on the man with whom I traded," he added.

"How was that?" the farmer asked his friend.

"The one who traded me this cow thought he was getting only a half section of land," said the farmer, "and he did not know he was getting 640 acres, or a whole section."

This joke that had been concocted by the farmer was intended to illustrate to his friends in town how much of a liability land had become in those days.

Year after year, the farmers who borrowed money to plant their crops were unable to even recover their expenses in a market that would not pay the cost of harvest. For a time it seemed that the larger the scale of farming, the deeper the farmer sank in debt.

Millions of acres of land were acquired by the mortgage companies, and the farmers lived on the lands they once possessed as mere tenants, farming the land on shares with the mortgage holders.

Landless Serfs?

Of a very serious nature was the passage of some of the Senate bills that passed more subtly in later years. One such bill was the Land-Use Policy and Assistance Act, Bill SB268. By a majority vote of sixty-four to twenty-one, this was passed by the Senate on June 21, 1973. On the surface, this 15,000 word bill looked desirable for times of crisis. But a deeper study of the contents caused some to raise their voices in concern or even alarm; these included the press, as well as the lawmakers who studied it.

The *Indianapolis News* declared,

The potential danger is obvious, since it is an axiom of economic life that he who controls the land can control the people who dwell on it.[264]

The *Lynchburg News* contained the comment,

When individuals within the confines of their communities are denied the right to determine the use of their land, but must conform to a national policy set mainly by others, they have lost the first and the most precious of their freedoms. For if government controls the use of the land, the people have been dispossessed of their own country.[265]

Senator Fannin of Arizona is quoted as saying,

The central element which clinches government control under Bill 268, is its ability to prescribe areas of "critical environmental concern."

. . . It is not folly to say that in some states every square foot of private and state land could fall within such a limitless definition.

The land already owned by the federal government is exempt from this act.

What we are doing here is embarking upon a program in which the federal government determines land use, not for the land owned by the federal government, but for all the private people. The land involved might be the smallest lot in the city; it might be a five-acre patch, or it might be a farm of 10,000 acres.

This bill would do great violence to our traditional American rights. Through the bill the property owners can be reduced to landless serfs, beholden to the lord of the manor in Washington.[266]

Living Off the Land

In the light of an impending crash, many well-meaning advisors send out their letters and formulas for survival, instructing folk to leave the cities and establish residence in areas where they have access to timber and water and space for gardens.

When asked if I favor such instruction, my answer is, "This advice is frustrating to many people."

Millions aware of the problems of the present day and the possibilities of a crash live from day to day on a salary that barely meets their daily needs for food and lodging. To suggest that such people move to the country is to torment them with a plan that is out of their reach. How can such suddenly leave their place of employment and find funds to purchase land in the country?

These might be ideal circumstances suited for a small percentage of people who are in the financial bracket or at the stage in life when they can leave the more crowded metropolitan areas for a quieter residence in a rural setting. But this does not apply to many young couples starting life together, nor many older who are still attached to their places of employment and residence in the city.

If there is evidence that there is a God who has spoken through His prophets concerning the days in which we live and the conditions we are witnessing, then by the same authority we have a Bible that declares His ability and faithfulness to care for those who trust in Him under any circumstances.

Anything of Intrinsic Value Is Better Than Paper

In looking back over history there are the vivid reminders of economies that have collapsed. In a single moment a stroke of the pen made worthless the paper that was used as legal tender or medium of exchange.

If one asked, "Would you rather have a piece of gold or an acre of land than money in the bank?", I would naturally answer, "If banks failed or money was suddenly rendered worthless, I would choose anything that was of intrinsic value in preference to worthless paper. In the drawer of my desk I have a file filled with the colorful currencies of many lands. Once they represented great value; now, their chief value is their power to remind one how transitory such money may be in its worth.

Your Security Is Better Than Mine

One day in New York I spoke on "The Death of the Dollar." In the audience that night was a man who had been chosen by the U.S. President to be on his staff as an advisor in monetary matters.

Later that same evening we sat down together in the restaurant of a New York hotel. I knew the man well. I had been his guest previously at the International Board of Trade, where he had been chosen from a thousand delegates of a hundred nations to be one of twenty men drafting rules for world trade.

He is a very knowledgeable man who traveled extensively in foreign countries and could well be termed a banker's banker.

After speaking of his investments and successes and the money he had laid aside for his children, he asked concerning my own personal financial status. When I told him I had virtually no money or securities laid aside for the future, it sounded like a financial failure. But the conversation did not stop there. I continued to tell how I came to a turning point in my life when I became totally convinced that man is a steward of material things that God has entrusted into his hands.

The clock ticked off the hours as we continued our conversation until almost 3:00 A.M. "If God is God," I said, "then His promises do not change with the rise and fall of the stock market nor the poverty or prosperity of a nation."

After handling considerable money in my earlier life, I told my friend how I decided to prove these promises made by Christ for myself. I went with my wife into postwar Germany when Berlin was 90 percent ruins. We went without either sponsorship or invitation when the nation was still struggling to climb back on its financial feet.

I told my friend how we had gone to Calcutta, and by personal choice took a modest dwelling on Tiljala Road among the poorest of the poor in one of the world's poorest cities. We not only witnessed miracles of divine care in meeting our personal needs, but also the blessing of God on the converts we won through the nightly services conducted in the tent on Royd Street.

The old Presbyterian cathedral that had been virtually abandoned on Wellesly Street was in sad repair, but we saw it refurbished and filled with people. We renewed the building with money that came from converts of our meetings.

Again in Kenya Colony in Africa we saw the continued care of God. We labored in Nairobi during the dark days of the Mau Mau uprising. We had come to Nairobi, as we had to Calcutta, without any financial backing from the homeland. Not only were our own needs met, but we saw a new church established there.

Seldom were the needs ever met in the same manner or from the same source. Life became ever more exciting. Sometimes we told no one but God, concerning the heaviest ventures that we undertook, but always our needs were met.

While we had by choice walked some lowly paths, we found to our amazement that God often seemed pleased to give us far more than we would have asked or desired. It was true of everything, including cars and homes.

In 1967 I had discussed with my wife the plan to sell our home in Pasadena, California, and give the money to world missions. On three separate occasions when it seemed that the cash buyer was ready to acquire our home, and we were ready to give the funds to the work of God, the sale was blocked in an unusual manner. So obvious was the miraculous nature of these experiences I was deeply moved, and said to my wife, "Verna, it is very apparent that God wants us to have a home, and cares more for the family than I do." When we found ourselves in the nation's capital with a lovely home free of mortgage and no other debts, I could only say it was miraculous. We had not made these possessions our goals in life, but had proved the Scriptures that said,

Give, and it shall be given unto you; good measure, pressed down, and shaken together, and running over. . . . For with the same measure that ye mete withal it shall be measured to you again. (Luke 6:38)

"Our first responsibility in giving," I told my friend in New York, "is giving to God. We must recognize His threefold claim on our lives; He created us, He sustains us, and His Son died for us. One day He will return to establish peace and order in a strife-torn world. But we need not wait for a golden day in the future, we can know His divine presence and care in our lives in the midst of turmoil and need. It matters not how dark those days may be."

When we arose to leave the restaurant and walked toward the lobby of the hotel my friend said, "Your security—your security is better than mine. I have money that will soon be worthless, and there is really nothing in life that one can say is truly secure. But you have proven that faith and obedience is security. You have seen it in India, Germany and Africa, and you will know this same care in our nation if it again passes through another dark hour."

Outside the door at the cab stand I said before parting, "While we all may vary in personality as individuals, the promises of God's divine care and provision are for all."

In the depths of the Great Depression my father demonstrated to his family and others that God's Word was true and the ability of God to care for those who put their trust in Him is limitless. One need not wait for a golden day when He rules on earth in righteousness and peace. Today, no matter what comes, He has promised:

My God shall supply all your need according to his riches in glory by Christ Jesus. (Phil. 4:19)

Notes

Elliott Roosevelt and James Brough, *Rendezvous with Destiny: The Roosevelts of the White House* (New York: Putnam, 1975).

[2] Ernest Lindley, *The Roosevelt Revolution, First Phase* (New York: Da Capo, 1974), p. 78.

[3] Ibid., p.87.

[4] Marriner Eccles, *Beckoning Frontiers* (New York: Alfred A. Knopf, 1951), p. 58.

[5] Antony C. Sutton, *War on Gold* (Seventy-Six, 1977), p. 81.

[6] Roosevelt and Brough, *Rendezvous with Destiny*, p. 50.

[7] *New York Times*, August 8, 1973.

[8] *Time*, March 6, 1978.

[9] James Dines, *The Invisible Crash* (New York: Ballantine), p. 5.

[10] Ronald Segal, *Decline and Fall of the American Dollar* (New York, Bantam), p. 69.

[11] *New York Times*, December 15, 1971.

[12] Peter D. Beter, *Conspiracy Against the Dollar: The Politics of the New Imperialism* (New York: Braziller, 1973), p. 44.

[13] *U.S. News and World Report*, July 29, 1963.

[14] *Washington Post*, November 13, 1968.

[15] Beter, *Conspiracy Against the Dollar*, p. 48.

[16] *New York Times*, September 4, 1972.

[17] *New York Times*, February 12, 1973.

[18] Sutton, *War on Gold*, p. 150.

[19] *Los Angeles Times*, December 13, 1974.

[20] Ibid.

[21] *Houston Chronicle*, June 12, 1974.

[22] *Glendale News Press*, December 6, 1974.

[23] *Newsweek*, June 6, 1978.

[24] *Orange County Register*, July 21, 1978.

[25] *Washington Star*, February 1, 1978.

[26] *San Jose Mercury*, May 23, 1979.

[27] *Washington Post*, March 29, 1977.

[28] *U.S. News and World Report*, April 30, 1979.

[29] *Newsweek*, October 30, 1978.

[30] *Sunday Mercury News*, January 29, 1978.

31 *Time,* June 12, 1978.
32 *U.S. News and World Report,* December 15, 1978.
33 *U.S. News and World Report,* August 7, 1978.
34 *St. Louis Post Dispatch,* July 7, 1978.
35 Abraham Ellis, *The Social Security Fraud* (New York: Arlington House), pp. 194-198.
36 Arthur M. Schlesinger, Jr., *Thousand Days: John F. Kennedy in the White House* (Boston: Houghton Mifflin), p. 105.
37 Lindley, *The Roosevelt Revolution,* p. 4.
38 Ibid., p. 247.
39 Ibid., p. 247.
40 Ibid., p. 101.
41 Ibid., p. 103.
42 Ibid., p. 239.
43 Ibid.
44 Ibid., p. 139.
45 The Stock Exchange Practices Reports, 1934, pp. 201, 202.
46 *Caught Short—A Saga of the Wailing Wall Street* (New York: Simon and Schuster, 1921), p. 31.
47 *Wall Street Journal,* November 11, 1927.
48 H.S. Kenan, *The Federal Reserve Bank* (Los Angeles: Noontide Press), p. 118.
49 Richard Ney, *The Wall Street Gang* (New York: Praeger, 1974) p. 16.
50 Ibid., p. 11.
51 Ibid., p. 18.
52 Ibid., p. 31.
53 Ibid., p. 31.
54 Ibid., p. 22.
55 Adam Smith, *The Money Game* (New York: Random House, 1968), p. 251.
56 John Maynard Keynes, "Economic Possibilities for Our Grandchildren."
57 Ibid.
58 Smith, *The Money Game,* p. 251.
59 Richard Barnet and Ronald E. Muller, *Global Reach: The Power of the Multinational Corporations* (New York: Simon and Schuster, 1975), p. 24.
60 Ibid., p. 187.
61 Ibid., p. 186.
62 *International Herald Tribune,* November 4, 1978.
63 *International Herald Tribune,* November 21, 1978.
64 Ibid.
65 Robert Engler, *The Brotherhood of Oil: Energy Policy and the Public Interest* (New York: New American Library, 1978).
66 Ibid., p. 37

67 *Time*, May 7, 1969, p. 71.

68 *Seattle Post Intelligencer*, May 29, 1979.

69 *Seattle Post Intelligencer*, May 31, 1979.

70 Ibid.

71 William E. Simon, *A Time for Truth* (New York: McGraw, 1978), pp. 56, 57.

72 Ibid., p. 60.

73 Ibid., p. 65.

74 Ibid., p. 61.

75 Ibid., p. 61.

76 Ibid., p. 225.

77 *U.S. News and World Report*, September 18, 1978.

78 *U.S. News and World Report*, September 25, 1978.

79 *International Herald Tribune*, June 16, 1978.

80 *Charlotte News*, October 31, 1977.

81 *Rocky Mountain News*, September 3, 1978.

82 Simon, *Time for Truth*, p. 173.

83 *International Herald Tribune*, March 11, 1976.

84 Ibid.

85 Kenneth C. Crowe, *America for Sale: An Alarming Look at How Foreign Money Is Buying Our Country* (New York: Doubleday, 1978), p. 36.

86 *Seattle Post Intelligencer*, May 29, 1979.

87 R. Buckminster Fuller, *Utopia or Oblivion: The Prospects for Mankind* (New York: Overlook Press, 1973), p. 243.

88 Wright Patman, "Other People's Money," *The New Republic*, February 17, 1973, p. 14.

89 *New York Times*, January 27, 1974.

90 *American Opinion*, February, 1974, p. 13.

91 "Super Giant Firms in the Future," *Wharton Quarterly*, 1968, Winter.

92 Barnet and Muller, *Global Reach*, pp. 52, 53.

93 Beter, *Conspiracy Against the Dollar*, p. 17.

94 Barnet and Muller, *Global Reach*, p. 96.

95 Ibid., p. 14.

96 Ibid., p. 18.

97 Ibid., p. 280.

98 *Washington Post*, August 21, 1973.

99 Barnet and Muller, *Global Reach*, p. 41.

100 Ibid., p. 29.

101 "Multinational Corporations," A Compendium of Papers, Washington, 1973.

102 *Growth of the Business World*, November 13, 1969.

103 Nelson Rockefeller, *The Future of Federalism* (Cambridge: Harvard U. Pr., 1962), p. 63.

104 Future of Multinational Corporations, May 1, 1972.

[105]Barnet and Muller, *Global Reach*, p. 41.
[106]Carroll Quigley, *Tragedy and Hope* (Angriff Pr., 1975), p. 325.
[107]Adolf A. Berle, *The Twentieth-Century Capitalist Revolution* (New York, Harcourt Brace, 1954).
[108]Charles P. Kindleberger, *American Business Abroad: Six Lectures on Direct Investment* (New Haven: Yale U. Pr., 1969), p. 179.
[109]Barnet and Muller, *Global Reach*, p. 16.
[110]*Los Angeles Times*, February 18, 1974.
[111]V.I. Lenin, *On Peaceful Coexistence* (Moscow: Progress Pub., 1971), p. 68.
[112]*The Congressional Record*, June 10, 1932, pp. 12595, 12603.
[113]Fuller, *Utopia or Oblivion*, p. 252.
[114]Ibid., p. 210.
[115]Quigley, *Tragedy and Hope*, p. 134.
[116]Ibid., p. 950
[117]John Kenneth Galbraith, *American Capitalism* (Boston: Houghton Mifflin, 1956), p. 65.
[118]Roosevelt and Brough, *Rendezvous with Destiny*, p. 113.
[119]Nietzsche, *The Will to Power* (New York, Gordon Pr., 1974), p. 30.
[120]Ibid., p. 30.
[121]Evans, *Let Europe Hear* (Moody Press).
[122]*U.S. News and World Report*, May 4, 1959.
[123]*Time*, October 23, 1978.
[124]*Time*, March 27, 1978.
[125]*New York Times*, July 8, 1973.
[126]*U.S. News and World Report*, July 17, 1978, p. 22.
[127]Roosevelt and Brough, *Rendezvous with Destiny*, p. 394.
[128]Ibid., p. 425.
[129]Ibid., p. 395.
[130]Ibid., p. 394.
[131]Ibid., p. 394.
[132]Simon, *Time for Truth*, pp. 30, 31.
[33]Paul Einzig, *The Destiny of Gold* (New York: St. Martin, 1972), pp. 34-36.
[134]Willard Cantelon, *The Day the Dollar Dies* (Plainfield: Logos Int., 1973), p. 116.
[135]Willard Cantelon, *Money Master of the World* (Plainfield: Logos Int., 1976). p. 59.
[136]*Time*, January 26, 1976.
[137]*U.S. News and World Report*, February 16, 1976.
[138]Cantelon, *Day the Dollar Dies*, pp. 114, 115.
[139]Roosevelt and Brough, *Rendezvous with Destiny*, pp. 427-430.
[0]Ibid., pp. 427-430.
[141]Virginia Cowles, *Rothschilds: Family of Fortune* (New York: Alfred A. Knopf, 1973), p. 207

[142] Ibid., p. 50.
[143] Ibid., p. 46.
[144] Ibid., p. 18.
[145] *London Times,* August 4, 1836.
[146] E. Corti, *Reign of the House of Rothschild* (Gordon Pr.), p. 245.
[147] Cowles, *Rothschilds,* p. 210.
[148] Ibid., p. 225.
[149] *New York Times,* November 1, 1970.
[150] Cowles, *Rothschilds,* p. 86.
[151] E. Corti, *Rise of the House of Rothschild* (Gordon Pr.), p. 64.
[152] Cowles, *Rothschilds* p. 60.
[153] Ibid., p. 118.
[154] Ibid., p. 162.
[155] Ibid., p. 17.
[156] Ibid., p. 41.
[157] Ibid., p. 105.
[158] Ibid., p. 129.
[159] Kressell, p. 1.
[160] Cowles, *Rothschilds,* p. 203.
[161] Ibid., p. 21.
[162] Ibid., p. 27.
[163] Ibid., p. 37.
[164] Amos Elon, *Israeli Founders and Sons.*
[165] Chaim Weizmann, *Trial and Error: The Autobiography of Chaim Weizmann* (Westport: Greenwood, 1972), p. 165.
[166] David Ben-Gurion, *Israel: A Personal History*, pp. 560-566.
[167] Ibid.
[168] Ibid., p. 795.
[169] Ibid., p. 797.
[170] Ibid., p. 67.
[171] Ibid., p. 161.
[172] Ibid., p. 63.
[173] Ibid., p. 378.
[174] Ibid., p. 846.
[175] The *Vancouver Sun,* November 15, 1975.
[176] Chaim Bermant, *The Jews* (New York: Times Books), p. 307.
[177] Ibid., p. 306.
[178] Amos Elon, *Israeli Founders and Sons.*
[179] H. Montgomery Hyde, *Stalin: The History of a Dictator* (New York: Popular Lib., 1974), p. 559.
[180] U.S. State Department Record, June, 1956.
[181] Hyde, *Stalin,* p. 495.
[182] Svetlana Alliluyeva, *Only One Year* (New York: Harper Row, 1969), p. 142.
[183] Ben-Gurion, *Israel: A Personal History*, p. 509.

[184]Roosevelt and Brough, *Rendezvous with Destiny*, p. 113.
[185]*U.S. News and World Report*, August 8, 1978.
[186]*Jerusalem Post*, March 26, 1979.
[187]Ibid.
[188]*International Herald Tribune*, April 6, 1976.
[189]*Newsweek*, June 12, 1978.
[190]Ibid.
[191]*Daily Telegraph*, May 2, 1978.
[192]*International Herald Tribune*, May 16, 1978.
[193]Ibid.
[194]*International Herald Tribune*, May 17, 1978.
[195]Ibid.
[196]Pipes, "The Goals of War," *Military Historical Journal*.
[197]*San Jose Mercury*, January 16, 1976.
[198]*Seattle Times*, January 25, 1979.
[199]*Seattle Post Intelligencer*, August 8, 1977.
[200]*International Herald Tribune*, June 6, 1978.
[201]*International Herald Tribune*, May 27, 1979.
[202]*U.S. News and World Report*, April 23, 1979.
[203]*Chicago Tribune*, October 8, 1976.
[204]Ibid.
[205]John Hackett, *The Third World War: August 1985* (New York: Macmillan, 1979), p. 30.
[206]Ibid., p. 304.
[207]Ibid., p. 317.
[208]Ibid., p. 315.
[209]Ibid., p. 3 1.
[210]Ibid., p. 316.
[211]Ibid., p. 324.
[212]*International Herald Tribune*, April 14, 1976.
[213]*International Herald Tribune*, June 5, 1978.
[214]*International Herald Tribune*, September 25, 1977.
[215]Cantelon, *Day the Dollar Dies*, pp. 132, 133.
[216]*Newsweek*, October 28, 1963.
[217]*Los Angeles Times*, September 29, 1973.
[218]Ibid.
[219]J.H. Brennan, *The Occult Reich* (New York: New American Library, 1974), p. 24.
[220]Ibid., p. 54.
[221]Trevor Ravenscroft, *Spear of Destiny* (Wehman, 1974), pp. 19, 20.
[222]Ibid., pp. 64, 69.
[223]Anne Frank, *Anne Frank: The Diary of a Young Girl* (New York: Doubleday, 1967).
[224]Ibid.
[225]Ibid.

226C.L. Sulzberger, *American Heritage Picture History of World War Two* (New York: Simon and Schuster, 1966).

227Ibid.

228*Charlotte Observer,* November 17, 1974.

229David Seltzer, *The Omen* (New York: New American Library, 1976), pp. 142, 106.

230*San Jose Mercury,* August 8, 1975.

231*Time,* February 20, 1978.

232Ibid.

233*St. Louis Dispatch,* December 19, 1971.

234*Los Angeles Times,* June 17, 1973.

235*Liberty,* July/August, 1978, p. 8.

236*Design News,* February 3, 1975.

237*Oklahoma City Times,* November 6, 1975.

238*Senior Scholastic,* September 20, 1973.

239Seltzer, *The Omen,* pp. 106, 105.

240*Oklahoma Journal,* July 10, 1979.

241Ibid.

242*Scientific Investigation of the Old Testament* (Chicago: Moody Press), p. 70.

243Peter W. Stoner, *Science Speaks* (Chicago: Moody Press, 1958), pp. 100-107.

244Ibid., p. 1.

245*The Evidence of God in an Expanding Universe* (New York: G.P. Putnam's Sons), p. 29.

246*Are All Great Men Infidels?* (Winnipeg, Canada: Hull Publishing Co.), p. 7.

247Ben-Gurion, *Israel: A Personal History,* p. 40.

248Ibid., pp. 18, 19.

249*National Enquirer,* January 30, 1979.

250*Time,* February 5, 1979.

251Ibid.

252Philip Schaff, *The Person of Jesus* (New York: American Tract Society), p. 40.

253Wilbur Smith, *Therefore Stand: Christian Apologetics* (Grand Rapids: Baker).

254Irwin H. Linton, *A Lawyer Examines the Bible: A Defense of the Faith* (Grand Rapids: Baker, 1977), p. 36.

255Simon Greenleaf, *A Treatise on the Law of Evidence* (New York: Arno Press), p. 13.

256Ibid.

257Ibid., p. 41.

258William E. Lecky, *History of European Morals from Augustus to Charlemagne* (New York: Arno, 1975).

259Wilbur Smith, *Have You Considered Him?* (Downers Grove: Inter-Varsity Press, 1970).

260Frank S. Mead, *The Encyclopedia of Religious Quotations* (Old Tappan: Revell, 1976), p. 56.

261Vernon C. Grounds, *The Reason for Our Hope* (Chicago: Moody Press), p. 37.

262Frank Ballard, *The Miracles of Unbelief* (Edinburgh: T & T Lark), p. 251.

263*Time*, October 25, 1976.

264Committee to Restore the Constitution, January 15, 1974, Fort Collins, Colorado.

265Ibid., p. 1.

266Ibid., p. 2.